UNWRECKED ENGLAND

CANDIDA LYCETT GREEN

OLDIE PUBLICATIONS

This edition published by Oldie Publications Ltd in 2010

First published in 2009
by Oldie Publications Ltd
65 Newman Street, London W1T 3EG
www.theoldie.co.uk

ISBN-10: 1-901170-14-4
ISBN-13: 978-1-901170-14-6

A catalogue record for this book
is available from the British Library

Printed and bound in the UK by Butler, Tanner & Dennis Ltd

UNWRECKED
ENGLAND

OLDIE PUBLICATIONS

Contents

Foreword

Many years before the launch of *The Oldie* in 1992, I was privileged to publish a feature in *Private Eye* called 'Nooks and Corners of the New Barbarism'. The writer was John Betjeman. He was eventually succeeded for a short time by his daughter, my very old friend Candida Lycett Green. The object of Nooks and Corners – which, I'm glad to say, is still in existence – was to highlight various examples of architectural vandalism of which there was never a shortage. 'Unwrecked England' was intended to redress the balance and to show the world that we were not merely knockers and were more than capable of expressing enthusiasm. No one is more capable of enthusiasm than Candida – an example to us all.

You will notice the beautiful engravings by the late John O'Connor dotted throughout the book. In the early issues of *The Oldie*, O'Connor's engravings accompanied Candida's 'Unwrecked' column. It is a pleasure to be able to reproduce some of them here.

Richard Ingrams
July 2009

Liverpool Cathedral – engraving by John O'Connor
See page 114

Preface

I am the archetypal Anglophile and remain, like Ruskin, ever faithful to 'blind, tormented, unwearied, marvellous England'. For me it is the most beautiful country in the world. It is also the most geologically complicated and in consequence provides an inimitable palette of constantly shifting colours: the shades of buff or red brick, or the depth of gold in the limestone vary from one village to the next. The cob and thatch country of deep-valleyed Devon is a world apart from the wide-skied marshes of pebbled and pantiled Norfolk, as are the lush Cornish 'hedges', thick with bluebells, stitchwort and campion, from the bleak curlew-haunted heights of the Yorkshire moors. The wildly differing local building styles serve as a wonderful gallery of England's unsung craftsmen. Every county is represented on the following pages for it would be impossible to do England justice without displaying the fierce local pride of each.

Richard Ingrams created this column for me seventeen years ago. He was actually paying me to indulge in my favourite pastime – exploring England. Inextricably woven through my childhood, the thrill of the journey and the possibility of finding some unknown wonder or half-remembered place is always with me. My mother's love of the landscape, for green roads, tracks, wayside flowers and shrubs, as well as for pre-history – barrows, earthworks, stone circles and cromlechs – became part of me. My earliest memories are of riding along the Berkshire Ridgeway, sometimes for a few days at a time. We diverted to deserted villages in tangles of undergrowth or to ghost-haunted barrows or never-forgotten houses, like Ashdown, stranded in the downs. We camped in sheltered combes and bought provisions in village shops. Early car journeys with my parents were long-drawn-out affairs and my father's love of place and of what he described as 'indeterminate beauty' meant that we stopped in nearly every town or village along the way to look at churches, houses and peculiar things – the crypt of St Leonard's Church in Hythe, for instance, where hundreds of skulls were crammed onto shelves; the Roman cave under a shoe shop in Royston; the secret, ivy-clad entrance to the Thames and Severn Canal tunnel. My father's passion for England was as much about its people, both past and present, as about its built legacy. As a result he made places come alive and inspired me with his love for them, often laced with funny stories about architects or eccentric owners: the absolute antitheses of fossilised academicism. When we were small, he rowed my brother and me from Lechlade along the narrowing upper reaches of the Thames, where yellow water lilies grow, to Inglesham. He led us through a messy farmyard to a church he knew we could not fail to like. The memory of its cool calm beauty stuck.

Travelling with my parents was a constant source of wonder and revelation. That their favourite hymners of the English countryside, its churches, towns and villages, are also mine is not surprising – John Aubrey, Oliver Goldsmith , John Clare, William Cobbett, Gilbert White, William Morris, Edward Thomas and Richard Jefferies to name a few. Since then I have added John Stewart Collis, Henry Thorold, John Michell and Roger Deakin to the list. They have all enhanced my view of England and opened my eyes to more.

This quest for the romance of England has never faded and the need for the long road before me has meant that, too lazy to walk, I have ridden or carted a few thousand miles across nearly every county in England. My friend Claire Murray Threipland has been the perfect travelling companion on countless journeys over the years. We talk sparingly and like the same things. We linger in villages, tying horses at the lychgate to look at churches such as Shobdon in Herefordshire or Kings Nympton in Devon. We find the most beautiful tracks, like the one which leads away from Mapperton in Dorset, or ride boldly up drives to unseen mansions. My longest journey across Derbyshire, Yorkshire and Northumberland was with Mark Palmer, whose love of bucolic England matches mine. I have found half the places in this book by horse and come upon them on unadopted tracks or lanes which often brought me to unfamiliar views of houses, towns or villages, rather than approaching them from the main road.

Apart from arriving at Crewe, Leamington, Somerton and Romney Marsh by train or barge, the rest I have been to with my husband Rupert, who shares my love of wandering along the way. On long journeys we try to travel as the crow flies, avoiding motorways and main roads and never without ordnance survey maps and Shell Guides. Our friend John Wells composed a song for a musical which echoes our thoughts: 'Sticking to minor roads and leaving our cares behind us, where nobody hopes to find us, we go. Happily making tracks and turning our backs on, things we know.' We like village pubs, staying in B&Bs and exploring counties we do not know so well, like Rutland or Lancashire.

I never stop being surprised at how wonderful England is when in the past its people, buildings and landscape survived turbulent change: devastation by the Danes, the Dissolution of the monasteries, the Enclosure Acts, the industrial revolution, the twentieth-century onslaught of motorised transport. Today the most disquieting threat of all is the loss of our natural farmland.

Opposite: High Force waterfall, County Durham. See page 90

Travelling by horse, as I have done for five decades, I notice every change in hedgerow vegetation and, apart from seeing roadside rubbish increase tenfold, I have been alarmed and depressed by the disastrous loss of wild flowers, and the depletion of bird, butterfly and bee numbers in rural areas which I have witnessed. Only the toughest weeds survive the chemical drift from sprayed crops, and nettles in particular, as well as docks, burdock and hogweed, now swamp our banks and field edges. When passing through cereal country the Ridgeway is often edged with legions of head-high nettles where once there were drifts of scabious, knapweed, mignonette, lady's bedstraw, lady's slipper and countless more flowers flickering with chalkhill blue butterflies. Only in the pastoral farming country of, say, Devon and Cornwall, in isolated areas like Salisbury Plain, or in government-designated Sites of Special Scientific Interest do wild flowers survive in their true numbers and escape being poisoned.

There may be other dark clouds looming as well: both urban and village communities face the devastation of their very fabric through the government's axing of post offices-cum-shops and the closing of fifty pubs a week because of the baron brewers' exorbitant rents, cheap supermarket beer and the smoking ban, while market stall holders, independent shop-keepers, fishmongers and butchers, etc. are being killed off by the supermarket and out-of-town hypermarket giants who provide both packaging and free parking. Gigantic Euro-sized lorries undermine our delicate network of small country roads and four-by-fours roar along, churning up our green byways. It may be in the English character to complain, not only about the weather but about the country going to the dogs, but despite everything, I am confident that our fighting and pioneering spirit will somehow overcome injustice and adapt to new things.

During the years I have been writing 'Unwrecked England' I have noticed changes for the good. Some planners have become more conscious of local styles and materials when making new-build decisions in rural areas. Organic farming and awareness of the need for biodiversity is on the increase, as are volunteer restorations of both lost railway lines and disused canals. DEFRA has been forced to take on board the need to revere nature and is giving grants for conservation strips around fields and for hedge-planting, when once, in a former guise, they gave grants to grub them up in order to create huge prairies. Some rural churches with dwindling congregations are beginning to bring back what used to go on in them before the village hall was invented by the Victorians – wakes, receptions, farmers' markets, meetings, kindergartens, concerts, etc.

The collection of articles which comprise this book does not dwell too much on self-consciously preserved places, but more on ordinary England, often battered around the edges and overlaid with modern development. From time immemorial, cities, towns and villages have evolved and new houses and cottages have been built in among the old and around the outer edges. Council houses, derided by aesthetes at the time of their building, are now an established part of our towns and villages and some have been listed. Sixties housing estates have settled over time, grown trees and developed idiosyncrasies. It is the *spirit* of a particular place which moves me, not so much the fine quality of its architecture. Stanhope, for instance, is not a pretty town, it is a strong-feeling one.

I now realise that the pastoral idyll we sometimes conjure, the '…irretrievable dream-England, / Visioned once in the warm light / Of half delusion half truth' of William Plomer's poem, never really existed, but I am more than happy with what is here. Tourists may find perfection in our show places of the Cotswolds like Bibury and Chipping Campden, but I prefer places which are off the beaten track. Even within earshot of a motorway's constant moan or a mere stone's throw from a gigantic conurbation such as Aylesbury, Warrington or Middlesbrough, as long as one is going at a leisurely pace, there are still beautiful bits of England to be found.

Candida Lycett Green
July 2009

Acknowledgements

Thank you so much to Julian and Isabel Bannerman, Terence Blacker, the Bledisloe family, Craig Brown, Sarah Bulwer-Long, Hugh and Grania Cavendish, Duncan and Sarah Davidson, Deborah Devonshire, Lawrence and Maggie Gordon-Clark, Maggi Hambling and Tory Lawrence, David and Sarah Kowitz, Claire Murray Threipland, Rory O'Donnell, Mark Palmer, Andrew Parker Bowles, April Potts, Cathy and Peregrine St Germans, Clio Turton, Theo Wayte, and Heathcote Williams.

Especial thanks to Christopher Sykes for his great photographs, his top company and his smooth, fast driving all over England in such a luxurious car. Also huge thanks for stalwart support and endless patience to Joe Buckley, Claire Daly, Sonali Chapman, Deborah Asher, Jeremy Lewis and James Pembroke of *The Oldie*, Jake Willott and Oli Terry of Computer Medicine Ltd, Justin Gowers, Rupert Lycett Green and all my progeny. And thanks to Richard for being the greatest editor of all.

This book is dedicated to Jasmine, who is on the glorious threshold.

SCOTLAND

WALES

14

Right: Craster
Far right: Wenlock Edge

Map key

1	Appleby, Cumbria	34	Godolphin, Cornwall	67	Salisbury Plain, Wiltshire
2	Ashdown House, Berkshire	35	Great Coxwell Barn, Oxfordshire	68	Salthouse, Norfolk
3	Batcombe, Somerset	36	Great Dixter, Sussex	69	Shap, Cumbria
4	Beverley, Yorkshire	37	Heale House Gardens, Wiltshire	70	Shobdon Church, Herefordshire
5	Blanchland, Northumberland	38	Heydon, Norfolk	71	Sidmouth, Devon
6	Blisland, Cornwall	39	High Force, County Durham	72	Sledmere, Yorkshire
7	Bottesford, Leicestershire	40	Holt, Norfolk	73	Sir John Soane's Museum, London
8	Bowthorpe Oak, Lincolnshire	41	Honington, Warwickshire	74	Somersby, Lincolnshire
9	Breamore, Hampshire	42	Iffley, Oxford	75	Southend-on-Sea, Essex
10	Bredon Hill, Worcestershire	43	Ightham Mote, Kent	76	Southport, Merseyside
11	Bredwardine, Herefordshire	44	Kelmscott Manor, Gloucestershire	77	Southwell, Nottinghamshire
12	Cartmel Racecourse, Cumbria	45	Kensal Green Cemetery, London	78	St Germans, Cornwall
13	Chatsworth, Derbyshire	46	Kimmeridge to Kingston, Dorset	79	Stamford, Lincolnshire
14	Chatterley Whitfield Colliery, Staffordshire	47	Leamington Spa, Warwickshire	80	Stanhope, County Durham
15	Chettle, Dorset	48	Leighton Hall, Lancashire	81	Stanway, Gloucestershire
16	Clun, Shropshire	49	Liberty, London	82	Swinbrook and Widford, Oxfordshire
17	Coate (Sapperton) Canal Tunnel, Gloucestershire	50	Linton-in-Craven and Thorpe-sub-Montem, Yorkshire	83	Tissington, Derbyshire
18	Cockayne Hatley, Bedfordshire	51	Little Gidding, Cambridgeshire	84	Torquay, Devon
19	Compton, Surrey	52	Liverpool Cathedral, Merseyside	85	Tregardock Cliffs, Cornwall
20	Cooling, Kent	53	Louth, Lincolnshire	86	Tring, Hertfordshire
21	Cottesbrooke, Northamptonshire	54	Lune Valley, Lancashire	87	Valley of Rocks, Exmoor, Devon
22	Cragside, Northumberland	55	Lydney, Gloucestershire	88	Wells, Somerset
23	Craster, Northumberland	56	Manifold Valley, Staffordshire	89	Wenlock Edge, Shropshire
24	Crewe, Cheshire	57	Mapperton, Dorset	90	Wensleydale, Yorkshire
25	Dorney Court, Buckinghamshire	58	Much Hadham, Hertfordshire	91	Whitby, Yorkshire
26	Ely, Cambridgeshire	59	North Bovey, Devon	92	White Horse Hill, Oxfordshire
27	Exton, Rutland	60	Oxford Canal	93	Whitehaven, Cumbria
28	Fairfield, Romney Marsh, Kent	61	Peto Garden, Iford Manor, Wiltshire	94	Widecombe-in-the-Moor, Devon
29	Forde Abbey, Dorset	62	Rame, Cornwall	95	Wilton's Music Hall, London
30	Fotheringhay, Northamptonshire	63	Ramsholt, Suffolk	96	Winterborne Came, Dorset
31	Frampton on Severn, Gloucestershire	64	Rendham, Suffolk	97	Winterborne Tomson, Dorset
32	Glynde, Sussex	65	Richmond, Yorkshire	98	Wistman's Wood, Dartmoor, Devon
33	Goathurst, Somerset	66	Rousham, Oxfordshire	99	Wooler, Northumberland
				100	Wreay, Cumbria

Appleby, **Cumbria**

The Eden Valley is England's Arcadia. Wide clear rivers loop and waterfall through red sandstone villages, small fields edged with hedgerow trees brim with buttercups in early summer, white pebbledashed farmhouses with black window surrounds are tucked into the folds of hills, their ancient farm buildings huddled around them, red squirrels inhabit the sheltering woods beside and the great fells loom in the background with ribbons of white water gills rushing down their gulleys.

Appleby lies in the valley's heart. Its mysterious, impenetrable castle, complete with twelfth-century gate tower and mansion house, crowns the hill, hidden from the world by high curtain walls. Leading from the castle's closed gates, tree-lined Boroughgate slopes steeply down to the church and the River Eden. Tall handsome stone houses go down either side, with little gardens in front, enclosed by iron railings. There are no chain shops on the market square and T E Ewbank, family butcher, dressed in a striped shirt, tweed trousers and smart braces, packs up several pounds of sausages in greaseproof paper for me. 'Remember they're Westmorland sausages, definitely not Cumberland.'

Appleby is famous for its Horse Fair, which has been held annually since the 1650s. In June the roadside verges are grazed bare by vanning horses, and all over Maulds Meaburn Moor there is evidence of travellers having camped on their way to this, the greatest congregation of gypsy horse dealers in the north of England. There is a party atmosphere all over Fair Hill above the town. Horses are tethered everywhere on banks and hillsides or tied to the back of pick-up trucks, fences and trees. Kettles boil on tripods over camp fires beside barrel-topped painted wagons. Dufton and Murton Fells rise behind, with the strange steep hills called 'pikes' before them. The A66 cuts through like a river, unnoticed and unheard below the noise of Irish horse-traders

holding Dutch auctions for saddles and bridles and the excited chatter of the crowd.

Piles of harnesses are sold from the back of horseboxes, whelks and crab sticks from stalls, and from lavish caravans and car boots cut-glass photograph frames, gilt-edged china decorated with coloured horses, gold-frilled party frocks for toddlers, Falabella ponies the size of spaniels, elaborate table lamps, toy tigers and saddlebags. Gaggles of young girls go strolling by, wearing high-wedged sandals, white satin miniskirts, dangerously low-cut tops and gigantic gold earrings, their bare midriffs bedizened. But it's along the straight lane that the real horse-trading is going on.

I sit on the bank and watch skinny young horses trotting at breakneck speed, their drivers leaning back in the small light sulkies and shouting to scatter the crowd or draw attention to their startling feats. Lurchers beside them, tubby men with rolled-up sleeves and braces, stand with their hands in their pockets watching the talent and discussing prices with earringed tattooed youths and racing enthusiasts. Sometimes more sedate turnouts drive up and down the lane – flat carts full of children pulled by hefty black cobs with flowing manes and tails, or gaily painted trade carts driven by old men in flat caps.

Back in the town and the evening sun, dozens of horses, ridden by children, sometimes two aboard, clatter down the slipway into the River Eden to wash and cool off. They splosh through the shallows and plunge and flounder through the deep pools by the red sandstone bridge. Through the churchyard, under the arcade and into the market square with its view up the avenue to the castle, there are benches outside The Hare and Hounds Inn. A Newcastle horse trader tells me about his favourite horse, May. 'I could yoke her and drive her fifty mile; she had bottle all right, that mare, not like some of them trotters back on the lane, they wouldn'a last a five mile.'

Right: cooling off in the river at Appleby Horse Fair

Ashdown House, **Berkshire**

It is Ashdown's setting which stirs the soul as much as the perfection of its architecture. To see the house for the first time it is worth travelling the track which leads up from Portway past Odstone Barn to Kingstone Down, on whose heights, two centuries ago, there was a racecourse.

Near where the finishing post once stood a footpath strikes off across a vast tract of plough to the brow of the hill where the ancient tufted turf has never been tilled and there is always lark song. Two lonely beech trees stand sentinel either side of a dead-on view of the chalk-white beauty of the house below, isolated among unending downland.

Ashdown was commissioned by William, first Earl of Craven, one of the richest and most chivalrous figures of the seventeenth century. When the plague was at its height in the mid-1660s he chose to build a house in the most out-of-the-way spot he could find among his vast tracts of land. He gave orders that there should be four-inch gaps under the doors so that germs would be blown straight through the house and out the other side, for he intended that Ashdown would be a safe haven for the 'Winter Queen', King Charles I's sad sister, Elizabeth. If not her unrequited lover, Craven was her staunch supporter during her long exile in the Low Countries. At one point she wrote to him: 'I have no more to eat, there is no money, no credit… This week if there be none found, I shall have neither meat, bread, nor candles.' He saw her right and when she was finally allowed to return to England during the Restoration he lent her his house in London while Ashdown was being finished.

Built of great blocks of local chalk with limestone dressings, the tall, ethereal-looking house was probably designed by William Winde, a soldier and amateur architect who had been brought up among the exiled Royalists. Ashdown certainly looks as though it has been plucked from a canal side in Holland and placed in these wild chalk uplands. Beautiful as it was, the Winter Queen never lived to see it. She died in Craven's London house, leaving him her papers and pictures, some of which hang in the house today. He lived for another thirty years and died a bachelor at the age of ninety.

Because William had built the much larger Hamstead Marshall near Newbury, Ashdown was never the principal Craven residence, but it remained popular for the great sport it afforded. Hunting was one of the family passions and from Ashdown's parapeted roof, with the huge cupola-topped lantern in its midst, flooding the central staircase with light, you could watch hare-coursing and the Ashdown Hunt in all directions. The sixth Baron Craven's wife, another Elizabeth, found an alternative consuming passion in the reigning Margrave of Brandenburg-Anspach and Bayreuth. She left Lord Craven in 1780 (having given him six children) and went to live in Germany with her lover. Lord Craven died the following year, the Margrave sold his principality to the King of Prussia and he and Elizabeth came to live at Ashdown for a short spell.

Over the centuries Ashdown has had a history of emptiness which adds to its haunting beauty. It is anchored to the downs by thick avenued woods. The place is redolent with ghosts of the past. Beyond Middle Wood, a twenty-one-year-old King Alfred rallied his troops in the valley fort known as Alfred's Castle and led the West Saxons to a glorious victory against the invading Danes in the Battle of Ashdown.

Right and inset:
Ashdown House

Batcombe, Somerset

Batcombe is dream England. It is a place you would be happy to reach by chance at the end of a long day's journeying. From Wyke Champflower, I had driven a horse and trap up Creech Hill in the drizzle by way of an age-old track which led up under a tunnel of nut trees growing on almost vertical banks of marmalade-coloured earth. At the top, the view across Batcombe Vale to the distant Somerset Levels was worth the climb. New plantings of carefully mulched hardwood trees on the roadside denoted some magnanimous landowner at work. The drizzle stopped and the birds sang. A steep narrow road, dark within its tree-shaded banks, led down to Spargrove, where there were vestiges of Roman habitation and terracing. Noble stables, ball-topped gate piers, walled gardens and a modest house tell of a larger, now vanished mansion. Overgrown box trees grow near the mill beside the little River Alham and a stone bridge leads over and on through open pastureland to join one of the seven high-hedged ribbon-like lanes which thread their way through hilly backwaters to Batcombe.

The village, built from the local grey-gold limestone, clings to the side of the northern slope of the steep deep valley. Way below, a tributary of the Alham meanders among cattle-strewn meadows and rooks wheel on the wind above the trees. On the highest mound, beyond the line of limes, the first sight of St Mary's Perpendicular church tower, sailing up above the ancient hills, brings a lump to my throat. It is glorious. Somerset church towers are the best in England. Batcombe's is more austere than Huish Episcopi's or Bruton's, but it is strong and right for its pastoral setting in this farming community. In his *Thousand Best Churches*, Simon Jenkins considers the interior a 'disappointment', but it isn't to me. Its simple roof and plain large square east window fits the scene.

Outside, a pleasing tangle of lanes interweaves between cottages and farmhouses with mullioned windows, one leading to the whitewashed Three Horseshoes pub. Dark and beamy inside, it is still privately owned and takes pride in its local Butcombe and Mine beers. The lunchtime drinkers are discussing the baron brewers wanting to theme all the pubs in England – how sad it is, how the new leisure industry is killing Britain… 'All this health kick,' says a tractor driver from Westcombe, 'with people wanting to spend their leisure time jogging. It's killing the pub trade.' There is also talk of Batcombe's legends – the phantom hound with a chain round its neck roaming Gold Hill at night, as well as a giant black-smith who appears if you call for him from the top of Burn Hill.

Further on through this dramatic switchback village, the five-bayed Georgian manor house overlooks a pastoral idyll of sheep grazing around an ornamental waterfall in the meadow below. From here, the old heart of the place, the lane leads eastwards, lined with ever-newer houses petering out into fields. At the dark bottom of the valley there is a particularly good farm, its hand-some house buried in sheds, dead tractors and old machinery.

Only a mile on, at the top of Seat Hill, you leave this intimate Somerset country of small hills and deep valleys and enter different terrain altogether in Upton Noble. The change is sudden and complete. The view opens boldly out on to a much grander and larger landscape where the estates of Stourhead and Longleat command huge tracts of distant woodland on the far horizon.

Left: St Mary's Church in Batcombe

Beverley, **Yorkshire**

Beverley is the sort of town you always hope exists. Yorkshire's inimitable spirit may have been diluted in some places but here it survives at full strength. The town is out on a limb and off the main tourist trail which favours the more glamorous York. In effect Beverley is like a small, reserved and quiet version of the latter. On the low-lying Holderness Plain, beside the deep-cut Beverley and Barmston Drain and the winding River Hull, which meets the Humber a few miles south, Beverley sports its own Minster, its own racecourse and a wealth of fine architecture. The Archbishop of York, John of Beverley, built the first church here in the seventh century, as well as Beverley grammar school, the oldest state school in England. It was John's miraculous reputation (the Pope canonised him in 1037) which rendered the Minster a privileged sanctuary and a centre for pilgrimage. What was once a quiet and remote spot became a thriving town. Beverley's consequent wealth, coupled with that of the local wool merchants, helped to build some of the finest ecclesiastical buildings in the land. Nothing can prepare you for the undiluted Gothic glory of the Minster. It is sublime: it lifts your heart and soul. As if that is not enough, there is still another architectural gem in the church of St Mary, which is just as marvellous as the Minster. Its proportions are perfect, and it was described by the church architect Sir Ninian Comper as 'the finest parish church in England'.

The town's fortunes fluctuated over the centuries but its cloth- and brick-making trades were constant, and by the eighteenth century the cream of the local rural gentry were building comfortable town houses here, Norwood House and Newbegin being among the showiest. The Assembly Rooms and theatre bustled with life. Much of the ancient grid of medieval streets had a Georgian face-lift and by 1802 even the gloomy Dorothy Wordsworth, who visited Beverley on a dark wet day, was 'much pleased with the beauty of the town'. However, a little later Anthony Trollope, who fought an unsuccessful election campaign here, dismissed Beverley as 'that most uninteresting town'.

Today its inhabitants know better. The Wednesday and Saturday markets are famous for miles around, as is the White Horse pub, commonly called 'Nellie's', which used to be run by six spinster sisters, the eldest of whom was Miss Nellie and the most regal of whom was Miss Dorothy. John Smith's of Tadcaster have now taken it over but it remains unchanged from the mid-nineteenth century when the gasworks came to town. Many of the town's shops are run by several generations of Beverlonian families: the wet fish shop on Wednesday market is run by the fourth generation of the Peck family who buy their fish every morning from Hull and smoke some of it themselves on oak or hickory.

From Beverley racecourse on its rise west of the town, the sight of the Minster rising gracefully from the clustered roofs of the town is breathtaking. The course belongs to the pasture-masters who look after the pastures or common lands of Beverley which form a verdant ring around the town – Figham, Swinemoor and the Westwood. The town paid a hundred shillings for the latter to the Archbishop of York in 1380 and racing has taken place here since the late seventeenth century. When it snows, the toboggan runs on the Westwood are bone-shakingly good and local children flock to them. The little hills are called names like 'Hill 60' and 'Majuba', presumably named after Boer War battles by school children of the 1860s.

Right: Beverley Minster

The Bishop's Palace Gardens, Wells, Somerset

Horas non numero nisi serenas – 'I count only the sunny hours' – is written on the sundials in Wells and, as Henry James commented, on whatever day you choose to go, 'it is always Sunday afternoon in Wells'. England's smallest city, no bigger than an average market town, Wells has always held onto to its ecclesiastical atmosphere. The glorious great Gothic Cathedral pervades all.

The hilly bit of snug Somerset near Wells is the calendar countryside of Perfect England. The switchback road from Bath to Wells leads up and over fat little hills of lush pastureland, patch-worked into thick-hedged or silver-walled fields. Red pantile-roofed farms are tucked into windless lees and curtained with cider apple orchards. There are herds of cows in every other field producing rich creamy milk to make bright yellow cheese. It is the sort of country that a child might draw, with semicircular hills stretching away into the distance, church spires rising from the dips and a round sun in the corner with stick rays coming off it. (Somerset means 'land of the summer people', because the Saxons used to bring their sheep from the uplands to graze here on the marshes.)

At Green Ore, a stone's throw from Priddy, where an annual horse fair is still held, the road to Wells strikes over the eerie, Stone Age-feeling Mendip hills across the old lead route down and down through high-banked ash-treed darkness into Wells itself, which rises out from the bright daylight on the level land below.

The Cathedral feels as gigantic and awe-inspiring as it was meant to feel when it was built from the twelfth century onwards. Here in the heart of Somerset, all seems well with the world, and despite its antiquarian picturesqueness Wells has not been fossilised. It is a thriving, bustling place. On the pavement in the market square the length of local heroine Mary Rand's Olympic long jump is marked out and, a little beyond, the cobbled 'Bishop's Eye' gateway leads past a gigantic cedar tree towards the Cathedral's matchless thirteenth-century west front, smothered with images of the saints.

Across the wide moat, where mute swans ring the bell below the gatehouse when they want to be fed, there is the secret, fortified domain of the Bishop's Palace Garden, surrounded by high walls.

Left: the ruins of the Great Hall with the Cathedral rising behind
Right: the mute swans in the Bishop's Palace moat

Fourteen acres of sweeping lawns are intermittently shaded by black walnut, gingko and Indian bean trees, and the most beautiful holm oak imaginable. The ruins of the Great Hall, once used for banquets, intersect the gardens. It became ruinous in the sixteenth century when its timbers and lead were robbed for another building. The remains were preserved as a romantic ruin in the mid-nineteenth century by Bishop Law.

If you climb up to the raised walk around the fourteenth-century battlemented ramparts above the moat, you can look out across an empty landscape of meadows, parkland and hills. The view in the other direction gives over the pantile-roofed town to the high line of the Mendips, and over the rose-red garden wall to the Cathedral and its hidden wonders of chapterhouse, cloisters, vicar's hall and vicar's close.

The Bishop's Palace, spreadeagled in the midst of the gardens, has grown organically around the thirteenth-century residence of Bishop Jocelin, who was granted the land by King John. Added to over the centuries by successive Bishops, it has ended with a Victorian Italian Gothic front.

Behind the Palace and past the Bishop's private chapel, a bridge leads across to the wells or springs from which the city derives its name. Four of them bubble up through the silt at the base of a wide pool which carries the Cathedral's reflection.

Blanchland, Northumberland

There used to be a railway which ran from Stanhope to Blanchland when the North Country coal and lead mining industries were at their peak. You can follow the abandoned line as it climbs along Horseshoe Hill, sometimes riding high on an embankment above the boggy bits of these moorland heights. It passes old quarries, disused mine-shafts and occasional coveys of grouse, which flutter up like tiny helicopters and then glide away down into another patch of heather. At Dead Friars, you join the unfenced road and start the long, slow descent to Blanchland through sheep-strewn uplands and over brown-water burns cutting their rocky ways through the hills. On a clear day, you can see for miles and miles to Hadrian's Wall and the pudding-shaped Cheviots on the blue horizon. Nearer the village, walled pastureland begins, surrounding small limestone farms. Foxgloves, harebells, moon daisies and hogweed swamp the wide verges of the old drove road, together with great sheets of rosebay willow herb, which will be shocking pink by August. Blocks of ink-black fir forests stretch away to the west along the banks of the Upper Derwent, and Blanchland lies hidden deep below, sheltered by softer woods and the enfolding hills. All along the lane into the village there are wild raspberry bushes.

Blanchland has always been so well hidden in its sheltered and secluded position at the bottom of the valley that on one of their many raids in the fourteenth century a band of Scottish marauders passed within a hundred yards of the village and never even saw it. Some hours later, in thanks to God for their deliverance, the monks rang a peal of bells, but the sound carried on the wind and the Scots returned to sack the place. When John Wesley came to preach here in the middle of the eighteenth century he described Blanchland as 'little more than a heap of ruins'. This was due partly to its constant sackings but also to the dissolution of the Abbey, when its heart was destroyed. Seven lanes and tracks lead down from the surrounding moorland to this beautiful spot where the Abbey stood. It was founded in 1165 by an extremely strict and self-denying order of Premonstratensian monks. They dressed entirely in white, which is thought to be the origin of the village name of Blanchland. After the Dissolution and the virtual abandonment of the place, it wasn't until the middle of the eighteenth century that the village found a new benefactor in Lord Crewe, who had made a packet from the surrounding lead and coal mines. An early philanthropist, he wanted to see his workers living in decent housing and created what is one of the greatest planned villages in England. The pale, grey-gold limestone cottages with stone-slab roofs seem to follow the old collegiate layout of the medieval Abbey and its buildings. The plan consists of a series of L-shaped courtyards, and you enter the large main square either through the old monastic gateway or from the southern end beside the river. The scale of it all feels utterly comfortable and the enclosure creates a kind of magic.

In the northern corner is the Lord Crewe Arms, which stands on the site of the Abbey refectory and guesthouse. What remains of Blanchland Abbey towers beside it. It serves as the parish church, and inside one wonderful arch still soars up under the tower.

Left: Blanchland

Blisland, Cornwall

If you come over Bodmin Moor by the southern slope of Hawkstor Downs, past barrows and bogs and the strange haunted henge called 'Stripple Stones', where sinister sundew plants wait to trap their prey and King Arthur's spirit hovers, a trickle of an unfenced road leads down through Treswigga to join a complicated cat's cradle of lanes. It is easy to get lost among them on the way to the village of Blisland, and if you were alone in the gloaming you might not feel entirely comfortable. Charlotte Dymond, murdered by her lover, a crippled farmhand named Matthew Weeks, in 1844, still walks the moors at night and the Beast of Bodmin has been sighted so many times in recent years that it is impossible not to believe in the panther-like animal's existence. From whichever direction you come, over the moor or through deep steep valleys where woods are white with wood anemones and clapper bridges lead across rocky-bottomed rivers, Blisland is suddenly and surprisingly there, perched on the slope of the hill above the woods. It is a place of pilgrimage whenever I am in Cornwall, not least because my father loved it so well.

Though the thin tall elms which he knew around the wide goose-green are long since gone, and there have been additions and a few new houses built on the edge of the village, it remains much the same as it was a hundred years ago. It is proper Cornwall: quiet, beautiful and out of the swing of the tourist route. The sparkling moorland granite is everywhere – glistening on chimney stacks, walls and around the mullioned windows. Seventeenth- and eighteenth-century cottages are scattered around the green, and the Edwardian Blisland Inn on the upper side serves food from nearby farms and seven local beers, including Sharp's Own from Rock, and Blisland Bulldog.

Down a tree-lined drive, a little out of the village, is the ancient granite manor-house of Lavethan, as perfect as they come, overlooking its own secret valley and small river, a tributary of the Camel.

It's the church on the lower side of the green that is the star of the show. The slate headstones in the graveyard slope away towards the edge of the churchyard and a deep, wooded ravine where buzzards glide at eye level. The square church tower is made of granite in blocks as big as chests of drawers, and a huge castor oil tree grows by the porch. The great church architect, Sir Ninian Comper, said that 'a church should bring you to your knees when first you enter it.' Blisland does. Granite arches spring from whitewashed walls; the barrel-vaulted ceiling is like an upturned ship with richly carved ribbing; the blue-grey slate and pale stone floor shines; a clear west window allows the sun to stream through; and a glorious painted wooden screen, red and green with barley sugar columns and gilded tracery, quite simply dazzles – perhaps the more so because it is so unexpected. The screen is Comper's and merges effortlessly with the architecture of this beautiful church, which has evolved over seven hundred years.

Comper was the son of a Scottish Episcopalian priest and his Anglo-Catholic upbringing had a lasting effect on him. His entire architectural career was devoted to ecclesiastical work, from new buildings to restoration and decoration. 'Man must first seek in youth for beauty by exclusion and he ends by finding it in inclusion,' he wrote, and then describes how the medieval Englishman would have seen the high altar: 'The holy place, no longer shut off to the eyes, he sees it through the screen as it were through a beautiful garden of paradise, for its mullions and tracery are painted with a thousand flowers…' His evocation of this vision seven centuries later is echoed at Blisland.

Left: the interior of
Blisland Church

Bottesford, Leicestershire

The Vale of Belvoir has long been pastoral farming country. Small hedged fields, wide verges and the vestiges of ridge and furrow gently undulate towards a distant view of Belvoir Castle on its sudden ridge of wood-topped hill. The Grantham Canal, built in the 1790s, winds through the Vale to Nottingham, and the old turnpike road travelling beside it now bypasses the beautiful village of Bottesford, leaving it calm and peaceful.

It is an unassuming place: in its heart it is all winding footpaths and streets of rose-coloured brick cottages and small houses with pantiled roofs. (The famous Bottesford blue pantiles were made here in the nineteenth century.) The River Devon (pronounced 'Deevon') laces its way through the village, widening into several fords, and a large orchard opposite the church is scattered with sheep and old fruit trees. The Victorian school has become the village library, the eighteenth-century rectory has been converted into retirement flats and the old station building now houses a large collection of mail-order stick insects. The Bull Inn on Market Street has a room devoted to Laurel and Hardy who stayed here in 1952 when Stan Laurel's sister Olga was its landlady. Resembling a large cottage, the Bedehouse stands on the corner of Devon

Lane and was built by a benevolent Earl of Rutland in the late sixteenth century to house local retired men. Further down the lane is a four-square Primitive Methodist chapel and an elegant eighteenth-century footbridge beside the deep ford. The handsome Regency police station on Queen Street faces Honeybee Cottage, whose garden is completely filled by an enormous magnolia tree.

But it's the great Perpendicular church of St Mary, known as 'the Lady of the Vale', which commands the scene with its 212-foot spire soaring into the Leicestershire sky, the highest in the county. I walked to it beside the red-brick rectory garden wall and crossed the Devon on an arched footbridge which was built in the early 1600s by the rector, Doctor Fleming. He nearly drowned trying to cross the ford by horse when the river was in spate and so determined to make the crossing safe for his parishioners. The tree-shaded churchyard is half-islanded by the river and a path cuts between pockets of primroses among a thousand headstones to the south door.

In this, their parish church, the chancel has been completely hijacked by the Earls of Rutland and their swaggering monuments, which are crammed in like an overcrowded antique shop. The high altar is barely visible and appears small in comparison. Eight consecutive Earls lie here in elaborate splendour, perhaps hoping for admiration from future generations: one even lists at length all the counts and dukes he has stayed with across Europe. The collection forms a wonderful showcase for the best sculptors of the day, from the stiff alabaster figures of the first Earl and his wife lying on their table tombs, carved by Richard Parker of Burton-on-Trent in the 1540s, to the sauntering seventh and eighth Earls, dressed in loose Roman clothing and carved in marble by Grinling Gibbons.

Two children kneel at the feet of the sixth Earl and his wife as part of the grandest tomb of all. The inscription beneath refers to the three Witches of Belvoir who are supposed to have been responsible for their deaths by 'wicked practice and sorcery'. The witches, Joan Flower and her two daughters, were servants at the Castle who were dismissed for pilfering and unseemly behaviour. The Countess of Rutland became convinced they were casting evil spells on her children. The three were sent to Lincoln gaol where Joan asked to eat bread and butter in an attempt to prove her innocence. If she was innocent, she would swallow the bread easily. She choked to death. Her daughters were executed on 16th March 1619.

Far right: the spire of St Mary's Church is 212 feet high
Inset: the Rutland monuments inside

The Bowthorpe Oak, Lincolnshire

Charles II so loved his oak trees that on the day of the Restoration, 29th May 1660, when he returned in triumph to London, he declared it a public holiday for 'the dressing of trees'. Oak Apple Day has been celebrated ever since in Royalist strongholds such as St Neot in Cornwall, where a leafy oak branch is placed in the church tower each year and the old branch taken down. The chant still rings out through the village: '29th May, Oak Apple Day, if you don't give us a holiday we'll all run away.'

Our love of oaks is absolute and their enduring qualities have often been linked with the character of the nation. Though seventeenth-century diarist John Evelyn may have been the first to coin the phrase 'hearts of oak', referring to acorns as a kind of health food to strengthen the body, it was David Garrick's famous shanty, 'Heart of oak are our ships/Heart of oak are our men', which made the phrase part of our folklore. The fashionable nineteenth-century garden designer John Loudon described the oak as 'the emblem of strength and duration, of force that resists, as the lion is of force that acts...' We fiercely defend any despoliation of the revered venerable trees and in 1995, when over a hundred old oak trees were felled in Windsor Great Park, a reporter likened it to 'chopping down the Queen Mother'. Famous ancient oaks are still venerated. Every county has its favourite tree: the hollow and hallowed Bound Oak at Farley Hill in Berkshire, for instance, or Kett's Oak near Wymondham in Norfolk, in whose shade Robert Kett rallied support for a rebellion against the enclosure of common land in 1549.

For its power to move, few trees in Britain can beat the Bowthorpe Oak. It is in the mild Lincolnshire transitional country of high-hedged lanes and gated roads which merge with wide, empty expanses of the dark-earthed, dyke-crossed fens. From the modest village of Wilsthorpe, with its pantile-roofed cottages and strange little eighteenth-century church, you can follow the long willowy lane to Spa Farm near where a thriving mineral water spa once stood, complete with Regency bathhouse and Victorian station halt. Cross the forgotten grassed-over railway line and follow the footpath up the rise to Bowthorpe just over the brow. Below the farmhouse and barns, a copse straggles up the other side of the shallow valley and huge willows and alders lean beside the upper reaches of the East Glenn, winding back towards Wilsthorpe. As you walk, dozens of brown hens scatter towards the great oak tree, the oldest in Europe: noble, aloof, solitary and stalwart, its presence filling the whole field and radiating an all-encompassing feeling of protection.

The Bowthorpe Oak is well over a thousand years old, and at forty feet round, it has the widest girth of any tree in Britain. There are records from the 1760s describing the hollow trunk being smoothed out by the then Squire of Bowthorpe, who created a room in which he could entertain twenty guests sitting down to dinner. The squires of Bowthorpe are long gone, as is their big house, but a later tenant of Bowthorpe Park Farm put a roof over the hollow trunk and added a door for shelter. He boasted that he could fit thirty-nine people in the tree with standing room only. More recently it has been used as a calf shed and as an annual tea venue for the children of the local Methodist chapel.

Right: The Bowthorpe Oak

Breamore, Hampshire

Breamore (pronounced 'Bremmer') is in the Hampshire of wide valleys between chalk downs, where villages cluster along river banks and houses are of rose-red brick. One half of the village clings to the River Avon and the relentless Salisbury to Bournemouth road. The other half, the most beautiful one, is scattered artfully around the great wide marsh, where bent willows shade the grazing cattle and occasional flocks of geese. The marsh is common land and the eighteenth- and nineteenth-century thatched cottages around its edges are half hidden in trees. Upper Street straggles further towards the downs and is shaded by evergreen oaks and a giant sycamore at Cross Trees Corner, beside which is a ravishing cottage with a flower-lined path leading up a slight incline to its front door. It has been quietly repaired over the years, unlike its semi-detached neighbour which has had an over-enthusiastic renovation complete with drive-in for the car. Towards the west of the 'upper' village there are some good brick farm buildings with

Right: the goose green at Breamore
Inset: a cottage at Cross Trees Corner

carthorse harness hooks still in place. Set back from the street is a grand little house with elegant iron railings and brick gate piers set perfectly symmetrically in a low wall in front.

A little way on, the finest Saxon church in Hampshire, built of whole flints with simple stone dressings around the doors and windows, stands in its brick-walled churchyard. Beyond a curtain of yews, the cedar-dotted park spreads out before a mellow red-brick Elizabethan pile, Breamore House. It looks to the distant woods of the New Forest on the horizon.

The house was completed in 1583 but its crisp perfection belies its nearly five hundred years. The poor ill-fated family of Dodingtons who built it and lived here had an awful time. William Dodington, anxious about a suit pending in the Star Chamber, 'went up St Sepulchre's steeple, threw himself over the battlements and broke his neck'. This suicide in broad daylight on 11th April 1600 caused a considerable sensation. As if this was not enough, their son William's wife was murdered by their son Henry in Breamore House itself. The house and much of the estate were sold in the eighteenth century to Sir Edward Hulse, whose descendants live here today.

It is worth every step of the mile-and-a-half walk through wonderful deciduous woods to reach the mysterious Mizmaze. At a crossing of tracks right in the middle of the wood there is a fine old tree with a divided trunk, known to generations of Breamore children as 'Twin Oak'. As you emerge from the wood an unspoilt and isolated tract of downland rolls out. Just ahead on the crest is a copse of yew and nut trees which secrete the Mizmaze – an eighty-five-foot-wide labyrinth cut into the turf. Nobody knows how old it is; perhaps its origins are connected with the twelfth-century Breamore Priory. There are only a dozen or more such mazes left in England, but in medieval times there were over a thousand across the country. Its pattern is much like many of the labyrinths found on the floors of great cathedrals all over Europe. As with the white horses of the chalk uplands, the Mizmaze needs regular weeding to keep it from becoming covered in grass and brambles. Local villagers traditionally did this job. A few years ago it was badly damaged by a gang of motorcyclists who drove all over it and cut it to ribbons. It has since been repaired and is now surrounded, like poor Stonehenge, with a fence.

Bredon Hill, Worcestershire

Worcestershire, one of the smallest counties in England, is only thirty miles wide by thirty-five miles long. It is a true Midland county of damson-coloured brick and black-and-white houses and cottages, secure and safe, with their skirtings of fruit trees which become mists of white and pink blossom in spring. Apple, cherry and plum orchards are everywhere – Evesham Wonder, Purple Pershore, Black Worcester – and pear trees have escaped from old orchards and seeded themselves in the hedgerows across the county.

Bredon Hill in the midst of the blossom is justly one of the most sung hills in England. If you approach it from the east, through proper plum country, you come to the glorious village of Elmley Castle, which is tucked under the hill's lower slopes. 'One of the most peaceful and comfortable of little places,' wrote Humphrey Pakington in Batsford's *English Villages and Hamlets* in the 1930s. 'May heaven preserve you from all molestation, most loved of all Worcestershire villages!' The twentieth-century housing estates which have leaked out into the fields since then are settled enough and feel part of the village. Near the church, the wide and comforting main street, with its tree-edged stream, opens into a little village square complete with the quaint black and white Queen Elizabeth pub, and beside it a lane leads up to Bredon Hill. Past half-timbered and stone cottages and the biggest pear tree I have ever seen, the metalled lane becomes a stone-based track which cuts through a high-banked russet-earthed tunnel of arching nut trees with ferns beneath. Suddenly the tunnel ends and you are out onto steep, ancient, tumpy ground where sheep graze under old hawthorn trees and somewhere unseen and undisturbed the violet click beetle crawls happily about. It is the sort of terrain which feels as though it has been like this since time immemorial.

Bredon is a leftover of the great Cotswold escarpment and looks as though it has been broken off and thrown out into the Vale of Evesham like a giant molehill on a lush and verdant lawn. To scores of generations, its heights were a harbour and stronghold and the ghosts of those times are here in the sacred standing stones, the earthworks, the remains of the medieval castle of the Beauchamps of Elmley and the huge Iron Age hill fort of Kemerton Camp which was inhabited for four hundred years. Age-old tracks cut deep into the hillside lead up and over to other villages which encircle Bredon's foot – Great Comberton, Eckington, Bredon's Norton, Kemerton, Overbury, Ashton under Hill, Conderton, Beckford. Mr Parsons, the squire of Kemerton Court, chose the prime spot on which to build his folly in the 1750s. From here, nearly a thousand-foot up, you can see what appears to be the whole of England spread below you into the blue distance. There could be no more moving nor lyrical description than A E Housman's:

In summertime on Bredon
The bells they sound so clear;
Round both the shires they ring them
In steeples far and near,
A happy sound to hear.

Here of a Sunday morning
My love and I would lie,
And see the coloured counties,
And hear the larks so high
About us in the sky.

When William Cobbett, who foretold the wrecking of the countryside, rode up Bredon Hill, he described its surroundings as being 'one of the very richest spots in England. These rivers, particularly the Severn, go through, and sometimes overflow, the finest meadows of which it is possible to form an idea.' Though the motorway whines beside the village of Bredon and industry spills out into the fields, I think he would still find that looking across his beloved England from these heights lifted his heart.

Left: the Iron Age hill fort and eighteenth-century folly on Bredon Hill above the Vale of Evesham

Bredwardine, Herefordshire

The Wye is one of our most beautiful rivers. It rises in the Welsh mountains and wends its way down to Chepstow and the Severn Estuary in great extravagant loops of slow-flowing, unpolluted water. By the time it reaches Bredwardine the Wye has become the stately and majestic river which, among many others, so inspired Wordsworth:

How oft, in spirit, have I turned to thee,
Oh sylvan Wye! Thou wanderer through the woods,
How often has my spirit turned to thee!

The graceful six-arched bridge which spans the Wye at Bredwardine was built by Thomas Davis of Hereford at a cost of £890 in the early 1760s. Thirty-odd years later it was put to the test when the worst flood anyone could ever remember left a trail of devastation in its wake. Every bridge on the upper Wye was washed away: Bredwardine's alone stood firm.

The brick, made in the local kiln, tells of the local soil. This is a country of red earth, high-hedged fields and box-framed half-timbered cottages. The setting of the straggling village on the west bank of the river is sublime. A toll cottage and medieval stone farm stand by the bridge, and up the steep slope are a red-brick Queen Anne inn called The Red Lion, a Victorian school, a scattering of cottages, and the Norman church in shades of mauve-coloured stone on a knoll above the river, half hidden down a short avenue of beech.

High sheep-strewn hills rise all-encompassing around the village and everywhere lush trees are scattered through the fields, as though some eighteenth-century landscaper had been at work creating an Arcadia. While riding in these hills, the Hereford-born amateur archaeologist Alfred Watkins had his vision. He realised that the whole country was crisscrossed with what he called 'ley lines', paths and tracks connecting up ancient monuments such as standing stones, churches, castles and Arthur's Stone, the neolithic burial chamber on Bredwardine Hill. His subsequent book *The Old Straight Track*, published in 1925, is still in print.

Bredwardine's most famous son is the diarist Francis Kilvert, who wrote so evocatively of nineteenth-century rural life. 'Why do I keep this voluminous journal?' he wrote. 'I can hardly tell. Partly because life appears to me such a curious and wonderful thing that it almost seems a pity that such a humble and uneventful life such as mine should pass altogether away without some such record

and partly too because I think the record may amuse and interest some who come after me.' Kilvert was the vicar of Bredwardine for the last three years of his life and lived in the pretty castellated vicarage behind the church which looks to the Wye.

Standing in the churchyard on a sunny Sunday morning you might still hear what he described in 1878: 'The whole air was melodious with the indefinite sound of sweet bells that seemed to be ringing from every quarter in turns, now from the hill, now from the valley, now from the deer forest, now from the river. The chimes rose and fell, swelled and grew faint again.' Tall, bearded and resembling 'a Newfoundland dog', Kilvert had a gift for inspiring affection through his diaries. He loved Bredwardine perhaps more than any of his other parishes. On 20th August 1879 he married Elizabeth Rowland and within a month, after a short illness, died of peritonitis. He was thirty-eight. The whole village was grief-stricken and people from far and wide and all walks of life flocked to Bredwardine to attend his funeral. The white cross marking his grave in the churchyard is inscribed with the words, 'He being dead, yet speaketh'. And he does. 'I have been trying to find the right word for the shimmering, glancing, tumbling movement of the poplar leaves in the sun and wind,' he wrote. 'It was "dazzle". The dazzle of poplars.'

Far left: Bredwardine bridge over the River Wye
Left: Francis Kilvert, vicar of Bredwardine

Cartmel Racecourse, Cumbria

Cartmel is probably the least known National Hunt Racecourse in England and also one of the most beautiful. It is surrounded by comforting, lushly-wooded hills and is set right beside the cosy village, with its grand priory church rising above stone roofs. It may not be frequented by many high-flying trainers – but then it is out on a limb, albeit a ravishing one, at the foot of the Lake District, where the mountains have turned into friendlier hills and the smell of the sea is on the air.

Racing has long been in Cartmel's blood; perhaps started by bored medieval monks from the priory who were said to race their mules along the sands on their way to Lancaster across Morecambe Bay. The track undulates unnervingly in this beautiful bit of north Lancashire, the chosen site of an ancient British camp. It is only a mile round, so nobody needs binoculars. It is either visible to the naked eye or obscured altogether when it travels through trees, more like a point-to-point course than a racecourse, sometimes getting very narrow, and at one point flanked by a solid Lakeland stone wall.

Being so tucked away it isn't surprising that one of racing's most brilliant coups took place in Cartmel in 1974, when Gay Future came in at 10-to-1 at the August Bank Holiday meeting. Thought to have been trained by an unknown Scottish permit-holder named Collins and ridden by an ill-considered jockey, the horse had in fact been sent from Ireland a few days before and stabled near the track, and was ridden by a top Irish amateur. The upshot was that the Irish betting team, who were hitting every betting-shop across London in what was actually a legitimate coup, lost out. Scotland Yard was called in and winning payouts withheld. It was by no means the first time that bookmakers had been outwitted over a Cartmel race, but it was the first time

that the police were involved. A national scandal ensued but the enormous crowds who come on summer and spring bank holidays never dwindled.

Cartmel village could hardly be bettered. It is just as Ward Lock and Co's Red Guide described it at the beginning of the century: 'A quiet place, a cathedral city in miniature, happy in the possession of a fine old priory church, one of the few which escaped the destruction at the Dissolution.' This great cathedral-like church, which dominates the village, is part of the vanished priory founded by William Marshal, Earl of Pembroke, towards the end of the twelfth century. Because it was also designated as the parish church for the local community of cocklers and fishermen at the outset, it was allowed to remain intact when all else was destroyed. The choir stalls and screen are exceptional and in the vestry is one of the earliest umbrellas in existence with a leather canopy. The church also owns a first edition of Spenser's *The Faerie Queene*.

There is a good five-bayed early eighteenth-century house near to the church of the calibre you'd expect to find in a cathedral close, and there are also pretty seventeenth- and eighteenth-century cottages on winding streets set beside the brook which runs through the village. Stand in Cartmel's central square and the views are lovely in all directions. On Priest Lane, Norman Kerr's long-established second-hand bookshop in the still unchanged premises of a Victorian draper's shop specialises in railwayana. What better station to call your own than nearby Grange-over-Sands, with its beautiful wrought-iron canopy painted apple-green and red?

Left: Cartmel Racecourse with the priory church rising beyond

Chatsworth, Derbyshire

The Peak District is a country of mountainous hills, dark peaty moors, of waterfalls and caverns, zigzags of loose-grit stone walls and deep and dramatic valleys. 'There are things in Derbyshire,' wrote Byron, 'as noble as Greece or Switzerland.' Chatsworth lies in the heart of the Peak, its own kingdom with its own palace, and when you cross the cattle grid into the park, London seems a thousand miles away. The pride of Derbyshire, the place appears to belong to all the local people who come to walk here, from Buxton, Chesterfield and Derby, from Matlock, Baslow and Bakewell.

From Calton Lees I walked down towards the great wide River Derwent which winds for almost two miles through the park. Here, where alders cling to the banks, there is a great weir of white water falling over a slow, curving bowl. The huge pool above is black like a silky sheet and almost still as it swings imperceptibly to the edge. Beyond the river the park rises up past ancient oaks to the steep heights of Stand Wood and Bess of Hardwick's Hunting Tower, like a lighthouse on the green cliff top. Northwards are the heights of Baslow Edge on which Big Moor stretches its almost pathless wastes.

Walking up-river the whole Elysian bowl of the park opens out. A second weir comes into view past a small copse where foxgloves cling to old tree stumps, and just beyond is the first view of one of the most majestic houses in England, dun-stoned and gilt-edged in the sun, with its window surrounds painted in gold leaf. It was here that Bess of Hardwick came in 1549 with her old husband, Sir William Cavendish. She built the first house, not a trace of which remains, but her descendant the first Duke of Devonshire began the existing one a hundred years later, and after a row with his architect completed the house to his own design in the early 1700s. The fourth Duke built the striking rusticated stables, and the Victorian 'Bachelor' Duke the substantial north wing.

On a level with the house, the Emperor Fountain shoots its astounding jet of water 270 feet into the air, while on the slope behind the house a spectacular cascade of white water falls down a long wide shallow stone staircase built in 1699. Joseph Paxton, the great gardener, and his boss, the 'Bachelor' Duke, were not only inspired by the romantic setting of Chatsworth but also by the infinite possibilities the water pressure from the hill behind

afforded. Paxton laid out the Stand Wood walks between 1834 and 1845, and the steep hill with its rocks and waterfalls was a perfect place for him to create endless surprises. Precipitous stone steps and leaf-moulded paths twist up past dripping steams and mossy crags, among ash, birch chestnut, wild cherry and rowan, sycamore, holly, yew, cedar, wellingtonia and spruce trees. Suddenly, as though you were in the African jungle, an aqueduct springs from the almost vertical hillside above and spills water onto moss-covered boulders eighty feet below. Its water flows along a conduit from the Emperor Lake in which water gathers from the moorland all around. Paxton harnessed the fall down the hill to create the pressure for the Emperor Fountain.

On a level with the lake, Bess of Hardwick's Hunting Tower crowns the skyline. It was built in the 1580s and remains unaltered. There is one room on each of its three floors and two turret rooms at the top. With its huge bow windows, it was designed for ladies to view the hunting taking place in the park below through the lattice panes. From up here it seems you can see all of Derbyshire. The estate is rolled out like an eighteenth-century map. In its midst, directly in line with the house, the great spire of the church built by Sir George Gilbert Scott in 1869 soars upwards above the model village of Edensor.

Left: Chatsworth House
Right: Bess of Hardwick's Hunting Tower

Chatterley Whitfield Colliery,
Stoke-on-Trent, Staffordshire

In the 1930s Chatterley Whitfield was the greatest colliery of all. It was the first in Europe to produce a million tons of coal a year. Back then there were four thousand men working there. Although the colliery was closed in 1978, the local community remain fiercely proud of this, the last survivor of the big Victorian coal mines. The buildings represent a tiny proportion of the colliery's true size. It extends a long way underground in all directions and joins up with the Wolstanton colliery further along the valley through a series of passages. With its empty winding-engine houses, lamp rooms, coal-washing and loco sheds, Chatterley Whitfield stands as a testament to one hundred and fifty years of engineering ingenuity and a monument to the bravery of the miners who worked on the coal face. Their spirit is here today.

The colliery lies on the outskirts of Stoke-on-Trent, beyond the narrow-necked brick bottle-ovens of the potteries of the 'Five Towns', the blackened Victorian church spires, the once proud civic buildings, the small parks, the rows and rows of back-to-back terraces and the scruffy brownfield sites. Nearby is the 'slatternly' landscape of Burslem, as Arnold Bennett described his hometown, with its historic Leopard pub. It was there, in the hub of Burslem,

that the Quaker pottery manufacturer Josiah Wedgwood and the engineer James Brindley plotted the building of the Trent and Mersey Canal, which in the end transformed the potteries and spurred on the industrial revolution.

Just over the hill the great landmark chimney of Chatterley Whitfield towers up from the heart of the colliery buildings in the valley below. Around its edges, the undulations of spoil from old workings and the remains of train tracks are lost in the white grass wasteland. In the distance the verdant hills of Staffordshire roll on to Derbyshire.

It feels as though the miners have only just left. The locker doors in the changing-rooms are half open; taps drip into the old pithead baths installed in 1938 by the miners' welfare committee and paid for by the men themselves. The stables from which the last horse hauled wagons of coal in 1932 became a loco shed, and train tracks lead in and out of the buildings and into the wasteland. In the Hesketh steam winding-engine house, red fire-buckets hang on the wall and a rusting notice reads, 'Men Descending. When the persons in the cage are ready to descend, the Banksman shall signal to the Onsetter and the Winding Engineers.' The names of the twelve Winding Engineers are printed below. In the nineteenth century, miners were lowered down the shafts in open tubs hooked onto winding ropes. Foxes live beside the Hesketh engine now, and a kestrel nests on one of the boiler chimneys.

Although small amounts of coal had long been extracted from Whitfield, it wasn't until the mid-nineteenth century, when the North Staffordshire Railway Company built a branch line up the Biddulph valley, that large investors became interested and its boom and bust history began. In 1873 the Chatterley Whitfield Iron Company, which owned blast furnaces and an oil distilling plant in the Chatterley Valley, were looking for large supplies of coal and bought Whitfield. They deepened the Ragman, Engine and Bellringer shafts to one hundred and fifty yards. But tragedy struck when a fire broke out through the misuse of an underground blacksmith's furnace, resulting in an explosion killing twenty-four men. The colliery's golden age began a decade later and it continued to prosper for nearly a century. The locals say that way down the 'drift' there is still one piece of solid coal, enough to last a hundred years. England's history is here at Chatterley Whitfield.

Far right: Chatterley Whitfield Colliery from Whitfield Tip
Inset: the deserted colliery

Right: Chettle House's
double staircase
Far right: Chettle House
was built in 1710

Chettle, **Dorset**

On the edge of Cranborne Chase, off a stretch of the blank, straight-as-a-die road between Salisbury and Blandford, a lane leads north-westward for three quarters of a mile to a wooded hollow. Here lies the lovely village of Chettle. Its seclusion is total. During the two hours I wandered round it, not a single car drove by. The stillness was extraordinary. Only the cawing of rooks, an occasional dog's bark or the cries of children playing broke the silence. Up a tree-lined track beyond the church, a great wood shelters the village from the western weather, while two Neolithic long barrows stand sentinel at each corner. 'Ceital', the village's Saxon name (meaning 'the deep valley between hills'), has harboured some form of tribal settlement since around 1700 BC. The present village is a mere spring chicken in comparison, but its settled feel is as old as the hills.

Across the thistled park, where Guernsey cattle graze, the glamorous red-brick manor house stands tall against huge trees. A long row of picture-book thatched cottages with kempt front gardens lines the lane and faces out towards the park. Further on, past an old orchard full of sheep under leaning apple trees, is the village shop: 'Purveyors of Provisions to the Chase Benefice… If it is not in stock we will try to get it for you.' The small, white-painted corrugated-iron hut, which also acts as the post office, is as unlike a supermarket as any shop in Britain. It might not stock avocados and balsamic vinegar, but it has everything I need: chocolate, cheddar cheese and postcards. Long wooden shelves sag with the weight of tinned peas and peaches. The cheery shopkeeper knows everything there is to know about Chettle. The whist drives in the village hall are once a fortnight, the carol service this year is going to be better than ever and, 'yes, it's a beautiful village, isn't it? There are no weekenders, only people who live here full-time and work locally. That's the rule. You know it's all owned by one family.'

The Chafins of Chettle were here for three centuries. Thomas Chafin famously commanded a troop of horses in defence of the crown at the Battle of Sedgemoor. (He later sent an account of the battle to his wife at Chettle. 'I hope to be home on Saturday sennight,' he wrote from London on 16th July 1685. 'The late Duke of Monmouth's head was severed from his body yesterday morning on Tower Hill about ten or eleven forenoon. Lord Grey will soone be there too. Blessings to the bratts. Soe farewell, my dearest deare Nan.') In 1710, the next generation of Chafins commissioned Thomas Archer to design a curvaceous gem of a Baroque house in place of the old one. It took twenty-five years to build, its front steps made of stone taken from a cave under the sea beside Portland Bill, its timbers cut from its own woodland, its bricks fired in the local kiln. Chettle's glorious double staircase is one of the most beautiful in the country. The last of the Chafins died in 1818 and the house was left empty. When a rich Wimborne banker, Edward Castleman, bought the derelict house in the 1840s, he modified it but managed to retain Archer's exuberant spirit. Castleman's practical descendants have divided the house into flats, retaining one for themselves, and turned the former dower house on the village street into a hotel.

Across the road from a handsome granary in a state of romantic disrepair and a weed-choked pond, stands St Mary's Church with its Perpendicular tower and its shining bands of flint and whitish Tisbury stone. St Mary's boasts the rare luxury of a priest in residence: in church terms, a Rural Peculiar.

Clun, Shropshire

Clun is a small town of grim grey stone among huge hills scattered with bilberries, Neolithic earthworks and Iron Age hill forts. The past rolls into the present in these hills, for the landscape has hardly changed and there is precious little plough – fields are still sprinkled with trees and there are oak and beech woods hanging on to steep hillsides. Clun itself sits on the convergence of eight roads and was for centuries a fierce bastion protecting the Salopians against the turbulent Welsh. At the time of the Norman Conquest Clun formed part of the extensive lands of Eadric the Wild, who led a revolt against King William and had his lands promptly confiscated. It was then given to Robert 'Picot' de Say and succeeding Lords of Clun added to Picot's original earth and wooden motte and bailey, rendering it a sturdy castle fortress. The remains stand high on a mound to the west of the town in a perfect defensive position, with the River Clun sweeping in a great bow around them. If you stand under the half-ruined tower it is like looking up at a modern skyscraper. During the 1990 Clun earthquake, described by a local as 'being shaken like a rat by a terrier', the castle's tower stood firm as a rock.

Since prehistoric times Clun stood on an important trade route which crossed the river here. The sturdy humpback bridge, with its five unequal arches and triangular stand-ins into which you can shrink from passing traffic, is fourteenth-century but its foundations are Saxon or, some say, even Roman. The local saying, 'whoever crosses Clun Bridge comes back sharper than he went', is still much quoted, so if you do take these steps you might be described as 'pert as a spoon' in Clun dialect, meaning sharp and bright. Other good Clun dialect words include 'taxy-waxy' for tough, stringy meat, to 'kwank', meaning to snub, a 'crod' for a short, stocky person, a 'butty' for a comrade or one of a pair (e.g. the left

shoe is butty to the right one), and a 'box-neck' for a somersault. Because of its remoteness, Clun's hundreds of strange words are kept alive and well by the locals.

On the far side of the river from the castle, up a short steep street, stands the solid Norman church with its square, fortress-like west tower, which suits the surrounding landscape. There are angels carved on the north-aisle roof and Welsh names on the gravestones among the yew trees in the churchyard. Beside the church is a good early eighteenth-century vicarage, and back across the river again a simple rustic Georgian town hall now houses the wonderfully eclectic Clun museum with its thousands of flint arrowheads. Perhaps the town's *pièce de résistance* is the magnificent Hospital of the Holy and Undivided Trinity, a refuge founded by Henry, Earl of Northampton, in 1614 for 'twelve poor men with a warden, subwarden, a nurse and a barber'.

In the last century there were fourteen pubs in Clun which were 'sniving' (swarming) with people on market day. By the 1920s there were eight and now there are only two. Having been a busy market town with a thriving shoe-making trade, Clun has long been known for its peace and quiet. The playwright John Osborne chose to live here and Sir Walter Scott stayed in Clun while writing *The Betrothed*, in which Clun Castle appears as La Garde Doloreuse.

The adjective in the following old couplet can be changed depending on how you feel:

Clunton and Clunbury, Clungunford and Clun
Are the quietest places under the sun.

Left: fourteenth-century Clun Bridge

49

Cockayne Hatley, **Bedfordshire**

Cockayne Hatley lies lost in far eastern Bedfordshire where the country rises and falls like a gently swelling sea. In a network of forgotten and disused lanes, this tiny dead-end hamlet, with an oasis of trees around the church on the crest of a rise, is stranded among vast fields of wheat, rape and peas. Mile-wide deciduous woods shield the land from the north wind. Once the hamlet was surrounded by the largest apple orchards in Europe. Mr Alexander Whitehead, who was responsible for planting them, bought the estate in 1929. A colourful entrepreneur, he used a form of pyramid-selling to build his orchards and invited people to become tree-holders for a subscription. He then encouraged his existing tree-holders to recruit others. By 1939 there were a thousand acres of Cox's Orange Pippins stretching to every horizon. The estate was later bought by the Co-operative Society who grubbed up the orchards in the 1970s because they were considered unprofitable.

For nearly five hundred years the estate had been the domain of the Cockaynes and their Cust cousins. In 1806 Henry Cockayne Cust became the 'squarson' (the squire and parson) of red-brick Cockayne Hatley Hall and the gingerbread-stone church of St John at its gate. Extremely devout, he had been dismayed to find, while conducting his first Christmas service, that snow was falling on the altar. Over the next twenty-five years he set about the restoration and ended with the most astonishing and eclectic display of Continental woodwork in the country. Ever since, the elegant triple-aisled church has been a place of pilgrimage to antiquarians.

In the early part of the nineteenth century and the wake of Napoleon's army, countless churches on the other side of the Channel sold their cast-offs to hovering antique dealers who, in turn, found a ready market in England. Henry bought the bulk of his church fittings from a Belgian dealer in Charleroi. They include the sensational seventeenth-century 'papal' stalls from the Abbey of Oignies, which was ravaged during the Napoleonic invasion of Flanders, and the lavishly carved panels on the chancel walls. Henry re-ordered the church, making collegiate-style stalls facing each other on either side of the widened aisle. He reset the brass memorials of his Cockayne ancestors in prominent positions, placed wooden angels in the roof, created screens with the lattice work of old confessionals, installed the hexagonal pulpit from St Andrew's, Antwerp (dated 1559), and the decorated organ carved with straggling garlands. Everywhere is a feast to the eye and the stained glass alone is worth a detour. There are some beautiful bits of thirteenth-century glass rescued from a Yorkshire church and set into the window of the north chapel.

The churchyard boasts a handsome monument to the poet and playwright W E Henley. 'I am the master of my fate; I am the captain of my soul,' he wrote in his poem 'England, my England'. As a young man he suffered from tuberculosis which resulted in the amputation of a leg. He was treated in Edinburgh where he met Robert Louis Stevenson. They collaborated on a number of plays and Stevenson used Henley to develop the character of Long John Silver. (Their friendship later ended in a bitter quarrel.) Henley was also close to J M Barrie whom he called 'friend', a term of address which Henley's four-year-old daughter Margaret interpreted as 'fwend'. She then adapted 'fwend' to 'Fwendy-Wendy'. Margaret died before her fifth birthday in 1894 and is buried beside her father, but her memory is immortalised in Barrie's *Peter Pan* as being the inventor of the name Wendy – a popular girls' name ever since.

Far left: the church of St John in Cockayne Hatley.
Inset: the 'papal' stalls from Oignies Abbey

Right: 'Pip's Graves' in
Cooling churchyard
Inset: the south-east tower
of Cooling Castle

52

Cooling, Kent

Cooling lies remote and windblown down on the level marshes of the Hoo Peninsula, which separates the estuaries of the rivers Thames and Medway. Up a narrow lane south of the village is red-brick Cooling Court, unassuming and beautiful and looking onto a muddy duck pond with its farm buildings crowded around. All is just as it should be in this unregarded corner of Kent. No one has got at it and tarted it up. There are no top-of-the-range four-by-fours out here. It is about as different to the posh side of Gloucestershire as England can get. There are only fruit trees in willow-lined orchards, a few scruffy ponies grazing in scrappy fields, poplars and the raw wind blowing off the sea.

No one goes there much, and the small population of the village has hardly changed over the last few hundred years. Slede Ooze, Hoo Flats and Stoke Ooze edge the southern border of the peninsula along the Medway, while Cooling looks towards the northern boundary of the snaking Thames. Across the water, gigantic tankers are docked beside great looming oil stores which tower over Canvey Island. It is the stretch of the Thames where the convict ship was anchored from which Magwitch escaped over misty Whalebone and Cooling Marshes to the churchyard in the eerie and unforgettable opening of *Great Expectations*. Dickens lived about five miles away at Gad's Hill Place, Higham, and described the place much as it is today: 'Ours was the marsh country down by the river ... I found out for certain that this bleak place overgrown with nettles was the churchyard; and that Philip Pirrip, late of this parish, and also Georgiana, wife of the above, were dead and buried; and that Alexander, Bartholomew, Abraham, Tobias and Roger, infant children of the aforesaid, were also dead and buried; and that the dark flat wilderness beyond the churchyard, intersected with dykes and mounds and gates, with scattered cattle feeding on it, was the marshes; and that the low leaden line beyond was the river; and that the distant savage lair from which the wind was rushing was the sea; and that the small bundle of shivers growing afraid of it all and beginning to cry was Pip.'

Pip had come to see the 'five little stone lozenges each about a foot and a half long', the graves of his brothers set beside those of his parents. Today they are known as 'Pip's Graves', though in fact there are thirteen stone lozenges, encrusted with gold lichen, most of them infant children of the Comport family of Cooling Castle.

Cooling is an ancient and important place – the life-blood of England has flowed up these lanes and tracks for centuries.

Everyone came through Kent to get to London, bringing new ideas from the Continent. The 'marshmen' of the Thames estuary in particular have been at the cradle of civilised England. King Harold gave the manor of Cooling to his brother, but when they were both killed in the Battle of Hastings, William the Conqueror gave it to his half-brother, Bishop Odo. The de Cobham family were lords of the manor by the fourteenth century, when it was fortified in order to defend itself from marauding Frenchmen. Massive curtain walls were built with corner towers in chequerboard stone and flint. Sir John Oldcastle married a de Cobham and lived in the castle at the beginning of the fifteenth century. He was a staunch supporter of the Lollards and by all accounts the original for Shakespeare's Falstaff. The castle was badly damaged a century later by Sir Thomas Wyatt, and from then on it fell into disrepair. The romantic ruins, set in a swampy moat and surrounded by willows and nettles, can just be glimpsed beyond the perfect gatehouse with its showy battlements and elaborate machicolations.

Cottesbrooke, **Northamptonshire**

I came to Cottesbrooke on a horse along tracks and lanes by way of the bright gold ironstone villages of Greens Norton, Cold Higham, Bugbrooke, Nether Heyford, Nobottle, Harlestone, Chapel Brampton, Teeton and Creaton, with its generous and glamorous green and spreading chestnut trees. I knew nothing of Cottesbrooke, but as the wide-verged road from Creaton dipped down towards a shallow and verdant hollow, the most sylvan picture of perfect pastoral England came into view. The church of All Saints stood on a slight rise with distant woods beyond and beside it the most beautifully proportioned eighteenth-century rectory imaginable, built of a stone the colour of honeycomb. The whole place exuded an air of tranquillity. A sign at the slow bend around the high red-brick garden wall of the rectory pointed away down the 'Gated Road to Brixworth'.

The fourteenth-century church, surrounded by tall Irish yews and with elegant Georgian box pews and a three-decker pulpit inside, was restored in the Wren-ish style in 1959 by Lord Mottistone, who was architect to St Paul's Cathedral. Sensational alabaster and marble monuments to the Langham family tell of their wealth and local benevolence. They came here in the seventeenth century and built a school and a long low cottage hospital on the Brixworth road. Then they built the present Cottesbrooke Hall and around it created one of the greatest sporting estates in all England, which it remains to this day.

There is splendour everywhere and if I were a braver rider I would have jumped my way across the park like Parson Legard, one of Northamptonshire's hunting clerics, who once, when conducting a funeral in the churchyard here, could not resist the temptation to join the hunt when it galloped past. He left the corpse beside the grave and leapt onto his horse which was tied to the gate and caught up with the field.

Beyond the church, the road is edged with young trees and passes the silvery stone entrance lodges to Cottesbrooke Hall. The gates are closed and the house, among lush gardens and sweeping lawns set with ornamental trees, cannot be seen. The drive leads away across an elegant bridge over a lake and into a seemingly boundless park. Along the village street there are cedar trees and pretty cottages – some of ironstone, some of buff-coloured pebbledash and some of brick. Thoroughbred horses graze contentedly in lush paddocks, and near the entrance of a well-to-do Victorian house, the last on the western edge of the village, is a sumptuous red may tree as big as an oak.

The unfenced road slices through wide cattle pastures and, in the distance, high hedges are trimmed in places for jumping over. Gated roads lead off in all directions, to Naseby, Guilsborough and Haselbech, across endless galloping grassland. Suddenly there is a glimpse, across a stretch of water and down an avenue, of the red-brick, stone-dressed Cottesbrooke Hall – early eighteenth-century by Smith of Warwick.

Here then is Jane Austen's model for Mansfield Park, amidst 'extensive plantations and pleasure grounds'. A stronghold of the old rural Tory values, it becomes Fanny Price's preferred home where she finds calm and order and 'no sounds of contention, no raised voice, no abrupt bursts, no tread of violence', which she had experienced as a child in her chaotic home in Portsmouth. When Fanny finally returns to Mansfield Park after a three-month absence, Jane Austen gives the landscape symbolic promise, and Fanny sees 'lawns and plantations of freshest green; and the trees, though not fully clothed… in that delightful state, when farther beauty is known to be at hand, and when, while much is actually given to the sight, more yet remains for the imagination.' The prospects of Fanny's life are reflected in her surroundings and the village of Mansfield, with its rectory 'half a mile distant', at its best, provides the perfect life.

Left: gated roads lead off from Cottesbrooke in all directions across grassland

Cragside, **Northumberland**

Cragside was the first house in the world to be lit by water-generated electricity. Rising like a Wagnerian castle from its steep ravine above the River Coquet, it is a hymn to the great inventor who built it, William Armstrong. The son of a Newcastle corn merchant, Armstrong trained to be a lawyer but in his spare time became obsessed with the idea of harnessing water power. Armorer Donkin, the benevolent mentor who employed Armstrong in his law firm, recognised a budding genius and allowed him time off to conduct experiments. Armstrong's innovative ideas coincided with the transformation of Tyneside after the Napoleonic wars into one of the most industrially advanced centres of the world, using coal, iron, steam and water as well as the navigable Tyne. Inspired by this heroic era of Newcastle's history, he eventually abandoned the law firm and began his own company, W G Armstrong. Both his scientific genius and his legal training helped him to bring about enormous industrial innovations at the peak of Britain's golden industrial age.

As a child he had often holidayed in the village of Rothbury in Coquetdale and his earliest recollections are of 'paddling in the River Coquet, gathering pebbles on its gravel beds and climbing among the rocks and crags'. His family used to joke that he had 'water on the brain'. In the 1850s, when his firm began to do well, he built a retreat on a spectacular site above the beautiful Coquet. He later employed the then little-known architect Norman Shaw, whose talent Armstrong had spotted, to enlarge his modest villa. Shaw travelled to Northumberland and wrote to his wife about the 'wonderful hydraulic machines'. On the skyline at Nelly's Moss, high above the house, Armstrong had made lakes to act as reservoirs for the main power-house 340 feet below. He also planted nearly seven million trees, which began to transform the rocky hillsides into a steep forest.

Shaw took fifteen years to enlarge and enhance Cragside and during that time never had one cross word from his employer, who was unfailingly described by his contemporaries as loyal, kind, considerate and easy towards his many friends. 'It will be very satisfactory working for Sir William as he knows right well what he is about,' Shaw wrote, and with Armstrong's constant involvement he proceeded to create a deeply comfortable and comforting house adorned with nooks and corners, panelling, verandas, look-out towers, bay windows and, in the dining-room, the biggest inglenook in the country. The level of detail with which Armstrong and his wife Margaret were concerned brought together of some of the most skilled craftsmen and artists of the day.

By the time Cragside became Armstrong's permanent home in the 1870s he was using it as a shop window for potential customers, fitting it out with every sort of device, from a hydraulically-powered lift to a kind of inverted lawn-sprayer which converted hydraulic pressure into rotary motion for the kitchen spit. When the Prince and Princess of Wales visited Cragside in 1884 it was the true 'palace of a modern magician', made even more incredible by ten thousand small glass lamps hanging all over the hillsides and lining the many winding paths. According to a contemporary account, 'the chateau itself was a blaze of light. From every window the bright rays of the electric lamps shone with purest radiance, and the main front was made brilliant by a general illumination.' The Armstrongs had no children. They left much of their wealth to Newcastle, its parks, hospitals and university.

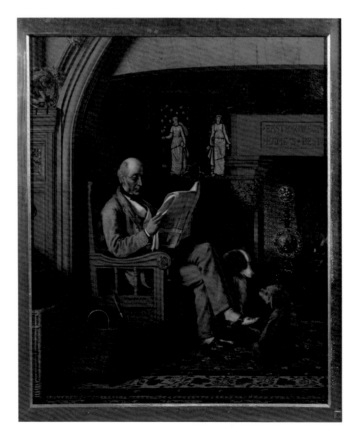

Main photograph: the west front of Cragside
Inset: painting of Lord Armstrong seated in the inglenook of the dining-room at Cragside (Henry Hetherington Emmerson, 1880)

Craster, **Northumberland**

Craster is famous for its kippers. For four generations L Robson & Sons have cured fish here in their original smokehouses built in the 1850s on this hazardous and unpredictable coast. They have survived hard times as well as surviving the EU regulators' costly and petty demands which at one time threatened to put them out of business.

Under steely Northumbrian skies I drove from the Great North Road through well-hedged Percy hunting country towards an ivy-clad folly high on Ratcheugh Crag, an eye-catcher and picnic house for the Dukes of Northumberland. They still reign over much of this beautiful and boldest of counties, where the bitter east wind whips off the North sea and a fierce air of feudalism and toughness pervades. Towards the sea and Howick Hall another ancient family has planted vast stretches of woodland and long tunnels of beech trees down valleys and all along the lanes surrounding them. The Greys have been here since 1319 (the second Earl Grey, pioneer of the Reform Act of 1832, was Prime Minister and also lent his name to the tea). The road dips down to a cove curling in from Cullernose Point and further on a beautiful Gothic archway with quatrefoil windows heralds the first view of Craster.

The arch was built in the eighteenth century by yet another ancient family: the Crasters of Craster, who have lived here in their pele tower house, secreted behind laurels and tall trees, since the twelfth century. More so than in any other English county, the same families still own their forbears' land and sometimes, as in the late Sir John Craster's case, demonstrate a sense of public duty. Born in 1901, he wore thick tweed knickerbockers, was a great supporter of the kipper industry, a county councillor, High Sheriff, a JP and wrote an inordinate amount of letters to the *Field* magazine about birds and the unusual habits of voles.

From its gorse-sprinkled heights the Crasters' house looks out over the huddled roofs of the plain little fishing village to the sea. Until the eighteenth century Craster village was on the hill near the tower, but in the early 1800s the present village began to evolve thanks to Craster family money. The herring yards took shape and in 1906 two piers were built in memory of Captain Craster, who was killed in action in June 1904 during the Tibetan Expedition. A small stream divides the village into the 'north side' and 'south side' and runs down to the deep black-shingled harbour. Sloping beds of glossy black Whinstone rock, scoured and polished by the sea, stretch along this dour, bladderwrack-strewn coastline. For centuries the seaweed was a valuable source of fertiliser and in 1301 caused Richard Craster to sue Richard Wetwang over the right of way by which Wetwang was taking his carts down to the sea's edge. This manorial right to the seaweed was a source of revenue to the Crasters until the mid-eighteenth century.

A little way out to sea, two islets known as Little Carr and Muckle Carr act as natural breakwaters and make Craster the safe haven it has always been. In the village there are black stone and whitewashed cottages, pleasing council houses down Heugh Road, the 'square' of fishermen's cottages, the Victorian church of St Peter the Fisherman, a memorial hall, and opposite L Robson & Sons' smokehouses The Jolly Fisherman pub affords a fire and a grand seaward view.

From the pub's window you can see a path leading out through a field, along the low cliff to the gigantic and menacing heights of Dunstanburgh Castle. It towers into the grey sky from its rugged black-rocked headland, the greatest, most melancholy and romantic fortress in England. When there is a big sea running the waves spray right over its curtain wall.

Far right: Craster Harbour, built in 1906 in memory of Captain Craster, who was killed in 1904 during the Tibetan Expedition. Inset: lobster pots by the harbour

Crewe, Cheshire

'Oh Mr Porter what shall I do? I wanted to go to Birmingham
But they sent me on to Crewe.'

Despite the jokes about delays at Crewe, despite working out anagrams of Crewe Station and coming up with 'Wait (no secret)' or 'Train woes, etc.', for me it is still a thrilling station to visit. A trainspotter's paradise, it is what Dungeness is to twitchers.

Set amidst lush Cheshire dairy country, Crewe remains the most romantic and practical railway town in the world. Look at it on a map and you will see the railway lines striking across Middle England towards it from six different directions. It looks like the middle of a snowflake under a magnifying glass.

In 1837 it was nothing more than a small stop between Warrington and Birmingham. At the point where the line crossed the turnpike road linking the Trent and Mersey and the Shropshire Union Canals, the railway developers bought land from the Earl of Crewe, whose Jacobean house stood nearby, and decided to call the junction 'Crewe'. The tiny village of Monks Coppenhall was swallowed up and, with the opening of the Grand Junction Railway on 4th July 1837, Crewe began to make world history. It was the first place to have its own railway hotel, The Crewe Arms, built in 1838. It was the first place to form a junction between more than two companies, and the first to have a completely independent railway system built around it to ease traffic congestion.

The purpose of the Grand Junction Railway was to link the four largest cities in England by joining the existing Liverpool and Manchester Railway with the projected London and Birmingham railway. The line, which was the first long-distance railway in the world, ran from Curzon Street Station in Birmingham to Dallam in Warrington. As soon as the station opened, it was seen to be a useful point to begin a branch line to the county town of Chester. A locomotive depot was built at the station to provide banking engines to assist trains southwards from Crewe up the Madeley Incline, a modest gradient which was a challenge to the small engines of the day. In 1842 the Grand Junction Railway moved its locomotive works to Crewe, and more and more houses were built to accommodate the growing workforce. The very best railway engineers were employed and, by 1861, the station had to be rebuilt to cope with the increased traffic. The town expanded still further under the leadership of John Ramsbottom, a Stockport man who was the locomotive superintendent for what had now become, through mergers, the North Western Railway Company – the largest railway company in the world. In 1871 he was succeeded by the colourful and brilliant Frank Webb, a vicar's son, who became known as 'the uncrowned King of Crewe'. By the 1890s Crewe had a thousand trains passing through it a day and the town's population was nearing fifty thousand. In 1903 another legendary railway man, George Whale, took over from Webb, but Crewe's power and glory in the railway world could not last forever. With the passing of steam, trains did not need to stop at Crewe to change locomotives. Myriad branch lines were axed by 'Butcher' Beeching and fewer and fewer trains terminated at Crewe. In 1985 the entire track layout was modernised, simplified and reduced.

In Crewe's heyday there was a strange and sad event. On 3rd October 1897, thirty-three years after marrying the actress Lillie Le Breton, Edward Langtry arrived at the station. It was three o'clock in the morning. He was penniless, confused and could not fathom how or why he had arrived at Crewe. He shuffled along to The Crewe Arms, whose manager had him taken away to an asylum near Chester. He died a few days later.

Left: Crewe Station

Dorney Court, Buckinghamshire

Leaving the imposing bastions of Windsor Castle and Eton College behind, you travel under the brown stock-brick railway viaduct, endlessly arching its way over this flat-as-a-pancake Thames Valley country, and take the blackthorn-edged road leading to Eton Wick with its mid-Fifties housing estates, blossom trees and concrete lampposts. Beyond it the road crosses a cattle grid on to a common scattered all over with groups of sheep, cattle, joggers, kite flyers and ponies. This huge wide stretch of pasture-land belongs to the lords of the manor of Dorney and its upkeep is settled by the villagers at the manor court each year, a satisfactory system which has been in place for centuries.

Dorney village, which lies in Buckinghamshire on the other side of the common, feels half-feudal and half-commuter-daintified. At a curve in the road, a drive through the laurel-floored woods leads to the heart of the place: Dorney Court and the village church – a perfect little pocket of timelessness among a sea of modern development. The M4 motorway whirrs half a mile away and the far-off fields of hay are under houses now. But there stands the manor house, an unperturbed survivor, across a little meadow and backed by the ravishing Tudor church tower. It is sublime – built of rose-red brick and timber it looks as though it is as much part of the landscape as the surrounding trees and the fat sculpted yew hedges which guard it.

Although the house epitomises 'Olde Englande' in the Stratford-upon-Avon sense, Dorney Court it is not over-restored and is more like a familiar old relation than a face-lifted film star. It has changed and adapted endlessly over the last six hundred years and its waving roofs and barge-boarded gables are woven together like tapestry. It really doesn't matter where the medieval starts or the Victorian begins because it has a completely homogenous feel and demonstrates that as long as a family loves a house it will go on living and adapting on a relative shoestring. The Palmers, who have owned it since the 1500s, have never had lashings of money: they have simply patched it up well and unobtrusively as and when necessary on the William Morris principle of restoration (Morris believed that restoration destroyed surviving buildings, and pleaded for 'protection in the place of restoration'.) Although the house is listed Grade I, the late Peregrine Palmer never applied for any grant money. He preferred to do things in his own time as his father had done before him, with builders who knew the quirks of the house as well as he did.

Inside, the layout of Dorney Court has changed little since the fifteenth century. A protective and cocooning feeling prevails. Each room feels like a safe haven, panelled wall to wall, and in the cosy parlour several Turkey carpets laid on top of each other and a huge open fire serve to keep the room snug. All around there is an eccentric mix of family treasures – from an early portrait of *Seven Eminent Turks* brought back from Constantinople by Sir Roger Palmer, an ambassador to Charles II, to the present Palmers' family dogs. There is the spectacular great hall with its original roof timbers which came from Faversham Abbey, and everywhere there is the ever-evolving story in linenfold panelling of the squirearchy of Palmers. There is a haunted bedroom which some members of the family have been too frightened to sleep in, and a pink Thirties bathroom suite in an oversailing bathroom where the pipes freeze up regularly. It's a lived-in and loved house, and feels like it. Ancestors have protested against the Elizabethan style in the past – a Victorian Palmer got fed-up with the low-ceilinged dining-room and made himself a mock William and Mary one, and an eighteenth-century Palmer tacked on a flimsy classical front which was later taken off. There was never enough money for a radical and irreversible overhaul.

Beyond the rambling house, the outbuildings, the old brewery and carthorse stables, stands the beautiful church of St James the Less. With twelfth-century origins, it remains calm and un-Victorianised and still has a family box pew – albeit half the height it was originally.

Far right: Dorney Court with its roofs and gables woven together like tapestry.
Inset: The Great Hall with timbers from Faversham Abbey

The Isle of Ely, Cambridgeshire

If you come by train from Cambridge the strange chessboard of unfamiliar Fens begins at Waterbeach. Beside the tiny halt there is an old orchard with beehives beneath the apple trees. The line is raised up above its floodable surroundings, waterless now, though Waterbeach was once described as a 'small fen archipelago'. The village's most famous son was Charles Spurgeon, who laid the foundation stone for a little brick Baptist chapel. He became one of the most famous preachers in England, drawing enormous crowds and baptising followers by the dozen in the Cam. A little to the north is a lovely group of buildings comprising Denny Abbey, which is set on what was once a tiny island in the archipelago. Much of the extensive Abbey remains have become part of a farm's steddings, converted over the centuries since the Abbey's demise. You can see it across the wide North Fen as the train trundles on towards Ely.

Over Stretham Mere, on either side of the track, fields of spinach stretch. Then cabbages, then huge empty plots of bitter chocolate-coloured earth. There are lines of poplars every so often to break the biting wind which blows in relentlessly from the North Sea. Lonely, plain little houses stick up abruptly now and then, as do red-roofed villages whose cottages huddle together among trees. Then suddenly, past Little Thetford, is the first view of Ely Cathedral. Even if you have approached it a hundred times before, its scale never ceases to astonish, and the mere fact that it was built from the beginning of the eleventh century by human hand alone, to the glory of God and not commerce, never ceases to move. In the early morning, when there is a mist on the Fens, the Cathedral rises like a gigantic ship on a pale sea and is probably as thrilling a sight as England can afford.

Ely Station is Cambridge's architectural twin with its fancy iron spandrels and biscuit brick. The steepness of the hill leading from it is surprising in this pancake countryside, but explains why such a great Cathedral was built here, for it was one of the largest islands in this once water-covered landscape.

St Etheldreda's monastery on the 'island of eels', of which she became abbess over thirteen hundred years ago, suffered under the Danes. (Etheldreda's popular name was St Audrey and the Pilgrims' Fair which took place at Ely was soon called 'St Awdrey's Fair'. The word 'tawdry' became part of the English language after hucksters sold cheap silk neckcloths at the fair and called them 'St Awdrey's chains' or, more commonly, 'tawdries'.) The monastery was re-founded in the tenth century and under the first Norman abbot the building of the Cathedral began.

The length and height of it are awe-inspiring, and the sheer bravery of building it dumb-founding. Imagine the windy night of 22nd February 1322: the monks were retiring to their cells when the great Norman tower fell into the choir and the earth shook all around. Alan of Walsingham then replaced it with the Octagon Tower – the most graceful feat of Gothic engineering imaginable. If you sit under it you can look up at the eight arches, four opening to the arms of the Cathedral and four to the clerestory. Off the north transept, a doorway leads to the supremely graceful Lady Chapel, built of the palest stone, like icing, and with huge clear-glass windows.

Near the Cathedral, the bishop's palace and a group of handsome houses surround the greensward of the 'college', and fine monastic buildings stretch along one side of the High Street. Close by, King's School is housed in spectacular medieval buildings with Norman undercrofts beside thistled parkland dipping down towards the level fenland.

Right: the west elevation of Ely Cathedral, also known as the Ship of the Fens

Exton, **Rutland**

Rutland is the smallest county in England: fifteen miles by fifteen. Over the decades, various government bureaucrats have tried to wipe it and its history off the face of the map by merging it with one of its larger neighbours, but Rutlanders have always fought hard to keep their independence. They are rightly proud of their county, the star of the Midlands. Its villages and towns are built in varying shades of golden marlstone or sheep-grey limestone and its undulating farmland is crisscrossed with quickset hedges and stone walls. Some lie drowned, together with the village of Nether Hambleton, beneath the gigantic sheet of Rutland Water created in the 1960s as a reservoir.

Exton is a beautiful place. If you approach it from Empingham along wide-verged lanes, the first sign of generations of well-heeled landowners is the dead-straight Barnsfield Avenue. Thick plantings of beech, birch, chestnut and sycamore line the way and later spill over the seemingly endless wall of honey-coloured stone which encompasses Exton Park.

The village, all of it built of the same honeyed stone, suddenly appears around a bend. Thatched cottages and pretty houses are perfectly grouped on all sides of the village green, which is shaded by towering sycamores. The Fox and Hounds pub stretches along one side of the green and a trout stream runs through the bottom of its garden behind. The main street winds on past an elegant circular pavilion on brick piers which once housed the village pump, towards the gates of Exton Hall, a Victorian pile well-hidden in its private Arcadia beside a sinuous lake. The village is surrounded by legendary hunting country. The oldest and most famous hunt of all, the Cottesmore, was first established at Exton by the Gainsborough family in the 1730s and the hunt has continued to meet on the village green ever since.

The church of St Peter and St Paul appears stranded half a mile away across the ancient park, but secreted beside it are the romantically overgrown ruins of the original seventeenth-century Old Hall, abandoned by the Gainsboroughs in 1810 after a disastrous fire. From outside the church looks forbidding but inside it literally takes your breath away. Triple-aisled and flooded with light through clear-glass windows, it houses the most spectacular collection of monuments. As you enter the south door a grand table tomb displays the stiff recumbent figures of John and Alice Harrington who lived at Exton in the early 1600s. In the south transept an elaborate show of marble obelisks, cherubs, Corinthian columns and a chicken-topped coat of arms frame the pious figure of 'Robert Keylwey, a distinguished esquire amongst civilians'. His daughter and her husband, who commissioned the monument, kneel at his bedside with their daughter Lucy. Nollekens has depicted eighteenth-century members of the Gainsborough family, but the most astounding monument of all is in the north transept, dramatically lit by the window beside it. Its florid swagger and preposterous scale beggar belief: baroque to the hilt, the white marble figures of the first Earl of Gainsborough and his fourth wife Elizabeth stand casually either side of a garden urn, their clothes draped artistically around them in Roman fashion. White marble swags of material are held above them by two black marble urns which in turn stand on top of beautifully decorated columns set with medallions of finely carved oak leaves and acorns. It's no wonder that Grinling Gibbons charged £1,000 in 1683 to produce the monument. Below the couple are two relief panels packed with former wives with their herds of children all got up in Roman togas. The inscription beneath is a terrible catalogue of stillborn babies, death in infancy and mothers dying in childbirth.

Far left: thatched cottages in Exton.
Inset: monument of the Earl of Gainsborough and his wife Elizabeth in Exton's church of St Peter and St Paul

Fairfield, Romney Marsh, Kent

Romney Marsh is another country altogether. Mysterious, windblown and eerie, it noses out into the Channel in low-lying watery flatness. Closely bound by the sea of which it was once part, its southern boundary leads along Camber and Broomhill Sands, through to great stretches of shifting shingle around Dungeness and then, with breakwater after breakwater jutting out into the waves, sweeps up past St Mary's to Hythe. Because the Marsh was dangerously near France and eminently vulnerable to invasion from Napoleon's army, the government of the time set about strengthening its lines of defence. First came the Navy, second the string of seventy-four Martello towers they built along the coast, and third the ambitious Royal Military Canal. It was begun in 1804 and cut along the bottom of the old cliff line for twenty-three miles from Seabrook to Winchelsea, effectively rendering the Marsh an island. Gun emplacements were placed at frequent and strategic points along the canal. Napoleon never arrived. Today swans and pleasure boats glide past patches of yellow water lilies and the myriad ruined defences, which were, in the end, used to police the many smugglers found in the Marsh.

Inspired by the churches, the pale light and distances of misted trees and low hills, the artist John Piper said of the area, 'What I really love about it is that it is all – ninety-seven per cent – atmosphere.' Romney Marsh is a colloquial name for what are really three distinct areas: Denge Marsh in the south, Romney Marsh proper in the north and east, and Walland, the emptiest of all, in the west. Crisscrossed in a delicate lattice work of dykes and ditches, the landscape of Walland harbours a scattering of isolated farmhouses at the end of long straight lanes, and an even smaller population than it did in medieval times. In winter the fields are awash with lapwings and golden plovers and in summer rare marsh mallow grows on the lush banks in secret pockets. The ghosts of lost villages haunt the place (the Black Death struck hard in the Marsh) but the church of St Thomas à Becket still stands strong above the flood level, stranded and alone in the emptiness of what was once Fairfield.

From homely Appledore the lane zigzags across the canal bridge and down the reed-edged lane to the vanished village, which was never more than a dozen or so dwellings of which two farmhouses survive. Edward Hasted, Kent's famous eighteenth-century historian, may have described Fairfield as, 'a most unpleasant and dreary place... far from what its name seems to imply', but the church has now become a place of romantic pilgrimage. For centuries it was approached by boat until the land was drained and exposed wide islands of pasture and a path on which to approach on foot. Romney Marsh sheep, which have adapted to the wet conditions, graze in the far distance between the channels and keep the sward around the church closely cropped. Even though much of the outside had to be rebuilt as part of the architect W D Caroe's gentle and sensitive restoration of 1913, the church has lost nothing of its power to move. The feeling of prayerfulness and calm is overwhelming. The massive timbers of pale washed-out oak, which form a simple barn of an aisle, the white painted Georgian box pews and three-decker pulpit all combine to create a perfect quietude. It is a place you do not want to leave.

Left: the Church of St Thomas à Becket in Fairfield, Romney Marsh

Forde Abbey, Dorset

Forde Abbey lies in dim, low-lying dairy country on the Dorset and Somerset border, where Hardy's Tess of the D'Urbervilles came up country to escape her past and fell so disastrously in love with Angel Clare. A valley away is the giant St Ivel creamery, the largest butter-producer in the south, whose swanky tubular buildings tower over Chard's forgotten railway station. In contrast, Forde rises serenely above the willows across from the deep-cut River Axe, the most complete Cistercian monastic building to survive – as a home – in Britain.

It has a head start in the beauty stakes. It is built of deep golden iron-stone from the famous Ham Hill quarry, which soaks up the sun and is etched all over with the palest grey lichen. The glory of the building's south side on a high summer's day is hard to beat.

The Abbey was founded eight hundred years ago and although its church has long since disappeared, the monastery still stands, transformed by the architecture of the sixteenth and seventeenth centuries into a rambling country house. The last Abbot, Thomas Chard, beautified the place, reconstructing the cloister and refectory, which remain as he left them. When Henry VIII ordered the Dissolution of the monasteries in 1539, the Abbot of Glastonbury was hanged from the gates for refusing to surrender. Fearful of

such a fate, Chard and his twelve monks decided to hand Forde over to the King. It remained empty and forlorn for a hundred years until in 1649 it was bought by Sir Edmund Prideaux, Oliver Cromwell's Attorney General, who set about transforming the Abbey into a sumptuous house. He made private family quarters at the east end and added state apartments over the elegant cloisters.

Created before English architectural taste became influenced by foreign styles, the building is wild and imaginative. The south front combines the last of our own Gothic with the first of the English baroque, all pulled together by a castellated parapet. Forde has nothing to do with Palladianism, which transformed the English architectural style of our grander eighteenth-century buildings into a measured tidiness. Forde remains uniquely inventive.

The back of the house is ghostly-looking with its jumble of turrets and towers and steep grey roofs from so many centuries – like a photographic collage of myriad bits of medieval buildings. Flights of swallows flew round the eaves and up above the chimneys when I came there on a hot August day. The undercroft, where the health-food café spreads its tables, is sprung over with Gothic arches of white- and gold-striped stone, and across the covered way a thirteenth-century wall painting of Christ on the Cross has been uncovered, the earliest Cistercian figure painting in England.

Wide terraced lawns climb the mild rise on the south side of the house to merge over a ha-ha with the oak-sprinkled park. A series of pools, originally made by the monks and restored in the eighteenth century, is joined by a series of waterfalls, which ends in a huge final pool reflecting the Abbey. The herbaceous borders beside it march into the distance, with Irish yews rising from them every so often. The perfectly ordered walled gardens contain a rampant mixture of all good things, from every conceivable summer vegetable to myriad agapanthus and a nice flashy bed of scarlet gladioli, orange montbretia, yellow dahlias, orange and red Iceland poppies, hollyhocks and love-lies-bleeding. A glamorous cockerel and many fat happy hens peck and scratch around the back courtyard, and towards the River Axe mown paths lead through long grass past patches of head-high Himalayan balsam. Beyond them, the occasional train from Waterloo whizzes through the meadow towards Exeter.

Far right: Forde Abbey, seen from beyond the ha-ha
Inset: the Abbey's castellated parapet

Fotheringhay, **Northamptonshire**

From wherever you approach Fotheringhay, you cannot fail to be startled by the grandeur of its church, St Mary and All Saints, which stands on a slight rise above a small and modest limestone village. You will probably come along small roads from Warmington or Oundle, Nassington or Woodnewton, but much the best way to get there is by boat. The River Nene snakes through the surrounding meadows on its languorous way through the rigid fens towards the Wash.

East of the church and closer still to the river is an uneven, sheep-grazed mound beside the farm – the sort of romantic brambled, hawthorned place which you might imagine to be the vestiges of a lost village. It is in fact all that remains of a large Norman castle with inner and outer courts and moats which commanded the ancient river crossing and surrounding district. Its destruction by James I (and VI of Scotland) was total. He wished to obliterate all evidence of its existence, so ashamed was he of what had taken place there.

Fotheringhay (pronounced with a silent 'g') is where Mary Queen of Scots 'passed out of th'entire into the hall within the said castle of Ffotheringhaie... with an apauled countenance stept up to the scaffold in the said hall and then and there made for her death.' Mary had been moved here from Charleby in Staffordshire on 25th September 1586. Her trial took place on 14th and 15th October and she was pronounced guilty of treason on 25th October. Queen Elizabeth signed the warrant for her execution on 1st February 1587. She was executed a week later.

If you stand on the grassy tump and look out over the quiet, undulating pastureland it is hard to imagine the macabre events of four hundred years ago. According to eye witnesses, when Mary was led to the block she was 'apparelled in a kinde of joye'. But the executioner did not have an easy time. When her head was eventually severed, he lifted it up by the hair to show it to the spectators – but Mary's hair was actually a wig, and so her head slipped out and fell to the floor, rolling away from him under the scaffold. Her dog, which had been hiding beneath her skirts, refused to leave and lay 'between her head and shoulders'. For the rest of her life, Queen Elizabeth can hardly have slept easily.

Fotheringhay had seen happier and more constructive royal times, if no less macabre. Edmund de Langley, the son of Edward III, planned a college here, but it was his son, the 'fatte' Duke of York, who actually founded it in the early fifteenth century. A few years later he was 'smouldered to death' at the Battle of Agincourt. His body was then boiled and brought back to Fotheringhay for burial. Richard III, our most enigmatic king, was born and spent the first six years of his life here.

The church used to be twice the size. What you see is all that is left of a large collegiate church – like those which are still intact at Warwick, Crediton or Arundel. As a result, the size and splendour of its great octagonal lantern look faintly out of proportion with the shortened nave, whose huge Perpendicular windows and elegant flying-buttressed clerestory belong to something much grander than an ordinary parish church. Inside, it is fan-vaulted and has a beautiful font and pulpit. In the field between the church and river the remains of the college are still tantalisingly visible, and in the village you can see what is left of two medieval inns, The New Inn, now a house, and The Old Inn, a row of cottages.

Left: the church of St Mary and All Saints in Fotheringhay, seen over the River Nene

Frampton on Severn, **Gloucestershire**

Frampton on Severn lies in a strange and forgotten area, stranded between the M5 motorway and the mile-wide River Severn. It is flat, watery vale country with views westwards across the river to the Forest of Dean and the mountains of Wales in the blue distance beyond. To the east, the sudden Cotswold escarpment rises from the flatness like a theatre backdrop. The skies are forever like a Peter Scott watercolour, for Frampton lies just north of Slimbridge, his bird sanctuary, and constant flocks of duck and geese fly homeward across the sunset just as he depicted.

One of the reasons why Frampton remains so sequestered is that most of the village lies in a cul-de-sac. A small road threads its way through the middle of a great wide village green almost three quarters of a mile long. There may be other large village greens but I know of none more lovely, nor more lordly. The absence of wires and roadside signage makes the whole scene pretty near perfect: a manor-house, a half-timbered barn, a court, brick farmhouses, two reed-edged duck ponds, groups of small houses and cottages spread generously along its edges.

It is called Rosamund's Green, after 'Fair Rosamund' Clifford, who was born at the ancient, rambling, half-timbered Manor Farm on the west side of the green. Rosamund's Bower, a projecting first-floor window which looks out towards passers-by, is said to be where Henry II first saw her as he rode by. He fell instantly in love and she became his openly acknowledged mistress until her untimely death in 1176 which was shrouded in mystery. One legend has it that Queen Eleanor led her to the middle of a maze by leaving a silken thread for her to follow and then poisoned her; another that she was murdered near Woodstock – bled to death in a hot bath. The pink-and-white striped *Rosa mundi* rose is named after her.

Descendants of the Clifford family still live at Manor Farm and still use a nearby fifteenth-century box-framed barn of silvery weathered-wood squares, with wattle and daub between, in which to store wool. Across the green from the farm, half hidden by chestnut trees, ilexes and a long wall, is Frampton Court, also owned by the Cliffords. It was built in the 1730s of bright golden limestone and is startlingly beautiful. An elegant sweep of steps rises to the front door at the centre of the main block, and there are small wings on either side with daringly high chimneys. If you look out over the low-lying park with its sheets of water you can imagine the five Clifford daughters who lived here in the nineteenth century and never married. They catalogued the flora of the area with exquisite watercolours and descriptions which were discovered in the attic in the 1970s and made into a book called *Frampton Flora*. In the garden, and visible from the green, there is a Strawberry Hill Gothic house at the end of a rectangular canal, in which it is reflected.

Beyond the green's end the road bends and becomes an ordinary village street until, as the houses begin to peter out, it stops at the beautiful church of St Mary, set alone and apart. A Judas tree hangs over the churchyard wall near an elegant gravestone carved with a weeping willow by John Pearce. A track continues on to Splatt Bridge, which spans the Gloucester to Sharpness Canal and swings open to let the barges pass through. Beside it is the canal keeper's cottage, like a little Doric temple with a pediment and fluted columns in perfect Cheltenham-style Regency. Then there is lonely marshland, merging with the muddy creeks and inlets of a swooping bend in the river Severn called the Noose. There was a murky mist hanging when I went and I was happy to turn back towards the village I knew.

Left: one of the village ponds on Rosamund's Green, Frampton on Severn

Glynde, **Sussex**

The great hills of the South Country
They stand along the sea;
And it's there walking in the high woods
That I could wish to be,
And the men that were boys when I was a boy
Walking along with me.

'The South Country' by Hilaire Belloc

If you walk up onto those great rounded hills between Eastbourne and Brighton, as Hilaire Belloc did, where beech-woods are sliced sideways by the wind and from whose heights you can sometimes see the sea, you will feel your spirits lifting. Resembling a long chain of huge soft pillows dented with curving combes, the South Downs are an archipelago of separate islands divided by rivers which run from the north down to the sea, and thwart their drift and flow. The Lavant, the Arun, the Adur, the Ouse and the Cuckmere cut through the chalk mass and create wide and gentle valleys between. These downs are different in character from those of Wiltshire, Berkshire and Dorset.

Sussex is a kingdom of its own. Saxon through and through, and as different from Celtic Cornwall as chalk from cheese. In the whole county, there is only one Celtic place name – the camp near Lewes, Caer Bryn or 'Mount Caburn', as it is now called. Nearby, on its south-eastern spur, lies the perfect village of Glynde. It's got everything the doctor ordered, even its own little station at the very bottom of the hill over the wide tidal reach of the River Ouse. Beyond the Scots pines beside the line, the handsome old railway hotel, The Trevor Arms, built of knapped flint, has old apple trees in its garden, lines of pewter tankards hanging along the ceiling beams, gaudy artificial flower arrangements on the tables, plates hung on pale green and cream walls, and a photograph of the greatest race mare ever, 'Sceptre, Queen of the Turf'.

Glynde is a famous stronghold of cricket, and from the railway bridge you can see the cricket pitch. (Nearby Firle, across the terrifying A27, boasts one of the earliest pitches in England.) Glynde, like Firle, is a feudal village. Many of the half-timbered and flint and brick cottages, together with a wacky smithy whose door is in the shape of a giant horseshoe, were built at various times by the Hampden family, who still own Glynde Place – a ravishing Elizabethan manor built of the local flint and a watery-coloured stone brought from Caen in Normandy. It's a magical place where a peaceful courtyard secretes a fig tree among cobbles, Japanese anemones and daturas. The beautiful eighteenth-century aggrandisements of a forbear, the controversial Bishop of Durham, William Trevor, are very much in evidence and include grand stables, fine Welsh dragons on huge brick gateposts and a small Palladian church looking as though it has been plucked from Verona. The Bishop was known as 'Good for Nothing' because he allowed everyone who came past his house to call in for a free tankard of homemade beer.

But Glynde's most famous son was John Ellman, an agricultural hero who farmed here from 1780 to 1829 and bred the famous flock of Southdown Sheep, bringing them to perfection. He lodged all his unmarried labourers under his own roof, and when they married he gave them enough grassland for a pig and a cow and a little more for cultivation. He built a school for his workmen's children, and although he didn't allow a pub to be built, he didn't object to beer being brewed at home. Considered the best sheep of their day for their meat as well as for their wool, the Southdowns began to lose popularity at the beginning of the twentieth century. Today they are designated a Rare Breed.

Left: The horseshoe door of Glynde Forge

Goathurst, Somerset

Goathurst is in the low-lying foothills of the Quantocks. From King's Cliff Wood, towering above the Somerset Levels, to West Quantoxhead, like the prow of a ship heading out into Bridgwater Bay, the sudden ridge of hills rises steep and often dark with woods. A track runs all along the heathery heights, while from it paths and lanes wind away down beautiful combes – Cockercombe, Seven Wells, Rams Combe – to a string of red sandstone villages sheltering in the shadow of these sometimes sombre slopes. 'The hills that cradle these villages are covered with ferns or bilberries or oak-woods, and walks extend for miles over the hill tops, the great beauty of which is their wild simplicity,' wrote Dorothy Wordsworth, who came to live here for a year in the 1790s with her brother, William, so that they could be near their great friend Samuel Taylor Coleridge. Coleridge lived in Nether Stowey, the showiest village in the Quantocks, which today harbours tourist-full tea shops and makes much of its famous son who wrote 'Kubla Khan' and the 'Rhyme of the Ancient Mariner' in his modest house on the village street.

Nearby, Goathurst remains a quiet backwater and is little visited, except by those on a quest for the lost park and pleasure grounds of Halswell House – once one of the greatest eighteenth-century landscapes in Europe and on a par with Stowe and Stour-head. Approached along an oak-lined lane, the village unfurls its modest houses and estate cottages, built mostly for farmhands, gardeners, builders and foresters who worked for the Halswell Tynte family. Their awe-inspiring monuments predominate in the great red sandstone church with its beautiful barrel-vaulted ceiling. At the west end of the village, a thatched *cottage ornée* punctuates the private drive to Halswell House and the lane winds on out of the village towards Enstone. Around a bend, the Temple of Harmony is suddenly there before you against a backdrop of foothills streaked with splashes of red-earthed plough. Overgrown and forgotten for a hundred years, it has now been restored to its original glory by the Halswell Park Trust. From up the slope, between groves of alders, a series of weed-choked ponds drops down in waterfalls to a final pool.

From the modest rise on which the temple is built you can look back at the tall, gaunt block of a house built by Sir Halswell Tynte in 1698, which is much admired by academically-inclined aesthetes. It is tacked onto a far friendlier medieval manor-house at the back, around which are vestiges of fishponds and a dovecote from those earlier times. All through the eighteenth century Sir Halswell Tynte's descendants proceeded to add untold grandeur to the hills behind the house by building cascades, bridges, temples, a rotunda, a stepped pyramid, a sarcophagus with garlands in memory of a horse, arbours, grottoes and rusticated buildings, many of them now lost, like the Druid's Temple, designed by Thomas Wright, 'the Wizard of Durham', a cosmologist, mathematician and garden designer who also dabbled in the occult and was popular with the posh people of the day. Sir Charles Kemeys Tynte, who employed him, would have been influenced by contemporary fantasists like the Duke of Beaufort, Wright's noblest employer.

Though the landscape is now splintered between different ownerships, a footpath leads through it, past the house and up a long slow climb to the top of the Quantocks. Almost at the top, in a black wood called the Thickets, stands the rusticated and beautifully restored Robin's Hood Hut, which is now managed by the Landmark Trust. From here there are views across the Bristol Channel to Wales and down over the lost and romantic landscape.

Left: the Temple of Harmony in the grounds of Halswell House in Goathurst

Godolphin, Cornwall

A few miles short of the end of England, towards the very edge of the west, Godolphin lies hidden in a doleful stretch of inland Cornwall, where depression still hovers and strange chimneys above redundant mine-shafts strike up through the brambles. Past Camborne, the two-storeyed tin-mining boom town, through the long straight Methodist-chapelled street of Praze-an-Beeble and out along treeless, telegraph-poled lanes, Godolphin's dark woods of soaring lichen-trunked beech and sycamore begin.

Somewhere in a patch of light, the great seventeenth-century granite house stands calm, once one of the grandest in Cornwall, and still as remote as it ever was. Everywhere there is an air of tranquillity that makes you want to linger.

Perhaps this has to do with the fact that there has been a settlement here for five thousand years. There can be nowhere in Britain which better shows the unbroken thread of human life continuing in one place, from the prehistoric hut circles, pillow mounds and Celtic field systems on the brackeny heights of Godolphin Hill to the remnants of tin mines in the woods around

the house – evidence of the Godolphin family's wealth.

Walking back from the hill, which still dominates the place, the track leads down under sycamores and bowers of honeysuckle clinging to bent hawthorn trees. Fern-smothered granite-block walls edge the fields. The stables and rambling barns, cart sheds, cow houses and piggeries are speckled with gold lichen. There are secret doors in high walls, campion and pennyroyal everywhere, swallows swooping under the eaves, dozens of brown hens scratching around and cats stretched along wall tops in the sun.

The house once had a hundred rooms and forty chimneys. Now little more than the strange and haunting seventeenth-century front remains, long and low with its eleven mullioned windows along the first floor and an open colonnade beneath, supported on great silvery columns of sparkling granite. A huge oak doorway leads into a courtyard where wisteria swamps castellated walls and the vestiges of the lost rooms. A perfect sycamore towers over the inner lawn.

The Godolphins were here from the fourteenth century, rising in fame and fortune, romantics and Royalists to the end – Sidney, the famous Elizabethan poet, his descendant, another Sidney, the famously honest Treasurer to Charles II who became the first Earl, and the last Godolphin, Francis, who died in 1766. He bred race horses at Newmarket and imported the legendary Godolphin Arab. His daughter Mary married Thomas Osborne, the Fourth Duke of Leeds, and the estate remained in the Leeds family. Let to tenant farmers, the woods became impenetrable and rats ran through the mouldering rooms.

Godolphin was brought back to the state of gentle perfection it is in today by Sydney Schofield, the visionary son of an American painter, Elmer Schofield – a friend of Julius Olson and the arty St Ives set – who bought his long-dreamed-of idyll in the Thirties. He and his wife Mary (sister of the painter Peter Lanyon) spent forty years restoring it, finding lost doors in neighbouring farms and Godolphin portraits in salerooms, including a John Wooton painting of the Godolphin Arab. The Schofields overlaid the place with the perfect degree of quiet, un-grand calm. The untouched Elizabethan garden layout – nine rectangular terraces with raised walkways and huge fishponds now filled with rosebay willowherb – add to the romance of vanished splendour.

Far right: the mullioned windows of Godolphin House together with the vestiges of lost rooms

Great Coxwell Barn, Oxfordshire

For me the Great Barn of Great Coxwell is a place of regular pilgrimage. I know of no more perfect building: everything about it is right. 'Unapproachable in its dignity,' wrote the poet, designer and socialist William Morris of the barn he loved so well. He considered it one of the finest pieces of architecture in England. It epitomises the very best of traditional arts and crafts, and inside it is like the most simple and awe-inspiring of cathedrals, standing stalwart and strong – a moving monument to the skills of the Gothic builders and carpenters who built it in the middle of the thirteenth century. One hundred and fifty-two feet long, forty-four wide and nearly fifty feet high, the sheer brilliance of its structure knocks many later buildings into a cocked hat. It has withstood the test of time like few others. Its original engineers were visionaries. The main load of the roof is carried by two rows of slender oak posts which have been so well framed together that they have not shifted,

nor needed replacing, in seven hundred years of resisting pressure and thrust. Likewise all the roof trusses. It is no wonder that this building has been an inspiration to artists and architects over the centuries. The small holes punctuating the walls, used to support poles during the barn's construction, let in shafts of sunlight on the earth floor like spotlights on a stage.

The barn also serves as a reminder of the huge wealth and influence of the medieval monastic orders, in this particular case, the Cistercians – or 'white monks', as they were called locally because of their unbleached woollen habits. A strict order, they forbade any kind of unnecessary ornament or decoration in their religious and secular buildings alike. They sought to reflect the peace and serenity of their life. At Great Coxwell they surely succeeded.

In the early twelfth century the Cistercians of Beaulieu Abbey had been given the Royal Manor of Faringdon – a large slice of Berkshire including several villages – by King John. Despite being based in Hampshire, the monks set up a grange here at Great Coxwell which was staffed by lay brothers who farmed the land of this, one of their greatest estates. The barn is the sole survivor of several farm buildings from that time, including a grain-grinding windmill. Since the Dissolution of the monasteries, the barn has remained in consistent agricultural use. The handsome Court Farmhouse was built close by in the seventeenth century and, together with the pond and the rise of Badbury Hill beyond, with its ancient earthwork, creates a serene picture.

The adjoining village of Great Coxwell has one foot in the Cotswolds and one in the Vale of White Horse. This is reflected in its long winding downward-sloping street of pretty cottages and houses, many of which are built of local random rubble limestone with brick dressings. The church of St Giles on the highest rise is surrounded by the most beautiful of graveyards. Here in unmown grass grow violets, primroses and snowdrops, and later bluebells, wood anemones, wild clary, scabious, birdsfoot trefoil and burnet saxifrage. Nineteen different sorts of butterfly have been recorded here, from Holly Blue to Small Copper. On the south side of the church are golden lichened gravestones leaning this way and that on a level height above the Vale and looking towards the long line of chalk downs on the near horizon. It's a wonderful place. The village street, complete with former Victorian school house, ends in a trickle of track, and beside it stands a handsome farmhouse.

Far right: the thirteenth-century barn at Great Coxwell
Inset: the interior showing the south door and the pressure support system

Great Dixter, Sussex

The garden at Great Dixter is tucked into the Kentish-looking side of Sussex where oast houses, apple orchards and huge oak trees abound. 'The wooded, dim, blue goodness' of the Weald which Kipling describes stretches away in every direction. Past weather-boarded, brick-and-timbered, tile-hung Hawkhurst, past watery meadows beside the River Rother and the much-filmed Bluebell Railway line, the village of Northiam sits on a slight rise.

Just out of the village, the manor of Great Dixter grows organically from its setting: clustered brick chimneys soar above the tiled roofs and barge-boarded gables. Well settled since the fifteenth century, with earlier beginnings, and seamlessly added onto by its Edwardian owner Nathaniel Lloyd and the architect Edwin Lutyens, you could never tell that a derelict yeoman's house from nearby Benenden was transported brick by brick and joined onto the original manor. Lloyd was a successful businessman, a master printer and the owner of a textile business in Manchester. So keen on golf was he that he re-designed the course at Rye, and so obsessed with the restoration of Great Dixter that he took up architecture. He asked Lutyens to lay out the gardens all around the house, using the site of the farmyards and original farm buildings as loggias and summerhouses. Lloyd himself designed a sunken garden with an octagonal pool in the early Twenties. Yew hedges, topiary, brick paths, pergolas, pools and orchards encompass, and almost bury, the house – beyond which, over Dixter Wood and down across the marshy valley to Bodiam Castle, the view reaches on to the heights of Bedgebury Forest and the blue hills of Kent beyond.

If Nathaniel created the canvas, it was his son Christopher who was the genius painter within it. Imbued with his mother Daisy's passion for gardening (she lived here with him until 1972), Christopher introduced planting schemes which made Great Dixter a true artist's garden: ever changing, fresh and inspired. Throughout his gardening life, which spanned over sixty years, he surrounded himself with young people and young ideas. The garden reflects this.

Although the 'bones' have the making of the conventional English idyll, complete with half-timbered manor, oast house and great barn, the planting is not what you would expect. There is no honeysuckle nor rambling rose scrambling up the red-brick walls,

no lavender spilling over paths. Instead, there are strange and exotic climbers like the lilac annual *Cobaea scandens*, startling giant dahlias of red and shocking pink, and vast patches of orange- and black-striped acanthus. You walk constantly into different worlds. Down the shallowest steps and into the high yew-hedged enclosure, you suddenly find yourself in a bit of Africa where giant shiny leaves grow as big as canoes, along with orange cannas and sumptuous, exotic rustling grasses as high as an elephant's eye. Walking round the garden is as uplifting as visiting a great modern art gallery.

Outspoken and provocative, Christopher Lloyd was one of the greatest gardeners of the twentieth century. His regular column in *Country Life* and his books, including *A Well-Tempered Garden*, produced an enormous following in their wake. 'Envy and ego-centricity are unnecessary limitations,' he wrote. 'If you cannot enjoy a plant seen in another garden because it couldn't grow for you... that's paltry.' Just two weeks before he died, in an effort to secure the garden's future, he appealed to the public: 'I don't want the place to become a museum... If it always remains loved and retains its own identity, everything else will fall into place.' Everything has fallen into place and those who now tend the garden continue in his spirit.

Left: Christopher Lloyd's colourful garden at Great Dixter

Heale House Gardens, **Wiltshire**

The valley of the Avon is no less lovely now than it was in 1826, when William Cobbett rode the length of it. 'Great as my expectations had been, they were more than fulfilled,' he wrote in *Rural Rides*. 'I delight in this sort of country; and I had frequently seen the vale of the Itchen, that of the Bourne, and also that of the Test, in Hampshire; I had seen the vales amongst the South Downs; but I never before saw anything to please me like this valley of the Avon … endless is the variety in the shape of the high lands which form the valley. Sometimes the slope is very gentle, and the arable lands go very far back. At others the downs come out into the valley almost like piers into the sea, being very steep in their sides, as well as their ends towards the valley … the land appears all to be of the very best; indeed the farmers confess it.'

Waving lines of pollarded willows and small straggling villages hug the river. The road Cobbett took meanders through West Amesbury, past silver chalk stone and flint-chequered houses, past Wilsford Manor, where the artist Stephen Tennant lived out his enchanted life and ended up as a Miss Havisham-like recluse, past the fat bastions of yew in the village of Lake and its tall, glorious gabled manor – Sting's private domain, high-hedged, high-walled, impenetrable: England evolving as it has always done, new money restoring the ramshackle houses built with old money – and always the downs undulating behind and melting into more downs where barrows abound and Stonehenge crowns the skyline.

Between Upper and Middle Woodford, the water meadows widen, the downs to the west gain grandeur and a chalk track ribbons away to an earthwork on the horizon. Opposite, a young lime avenue leads away across a sheep-strewn field and, there below, hidden until you are almost upon it, stands a red-brick and stone-dressed manor-house beside the river, surrounded by the most entrancing gardens imaginable.

Heale House, apparently a perfect late seventeenth-century house, was in fact restored after a fire and aggrandised by its new owner, Louis Greville, at the turn of the last century. He employed the gifted Arts and Crafts architect Detmar Blow to restore the house, and the garden designer Harold Peto to make the most of this gentle slope of ground within a lazy loop of the trout-filled Avon. He planted yew hedges and laid down stone terraces, balustrades and wide, shallow steps, now lichen- and moss-encrusted. Artful additions, elaborations and new plantings by subsequent generations have made Heale Gardens a magic place, worth dipping into every time you pass. It is just the right scale, a garden in which you feel happy alone. For the most part it is the comforting English idyll – tunnels of apple trees through the walled vegetable garden, musk roses against faded red brick – but there is also a Japanese garden with an islanded tea house painted scarlet. It stands over a channel dug in 1690 as part of the new water meadow irrigation system designed by Dutch engineers. The system still works and is in use at Court Farm, two miles down the valley.

Even in winter there are beautiful plants and shrubs in bloom – witch hazels, hellebores, mahonia, winter jasmine and honeysuckle – but best of all, on a walk which they call 'the cut', a winding incline unfurls to the water meadows and reveals sheets of snowdrops and aconites on its high banks.

Right: Heale House is set in gardens originally designed and laid out by Harold Peto

Heydon, **Norfolk**

Heydon is little known and on the way to nowhere. Quiet and undisturbed, it lies in some of the richest landscape for miles around. Across so much of East Anglia in particular, huge tracts of countryside were devastated in the mid-twentieth century by agribusiness and the government incentives to rip out hedges. Fields the length of a furlong – as far as a horse could pull the plough without a breather – went out of the window and protection from the wind whipping off the North Sea was gone for good. Today there are grants to put back hedges, but it is impossible to recreate overnight the idiosyncratic texture which nature and good husbandry create over centuries. The family who farm the land around Heydon were visionary. They hung onto their hedges while all about them were losing theirs. They are now the envy of all their neighbours. Heydon shines, anchored by trees and woods and secret dells and well-cared-for hedges.

A wood and a park away from the main Norwich-to-Holt road, you turn off past Dog Corner and thickly bluebelled Newhall Wood to the dead-end turning for the village. Just before it, there is a glimpse of the lovely gabled Grange, lying low down an old chestnut avenue. The village is pretty near perfect, but it is not quaint like some villages. Heydon is a working village which manages to retain the ideal degree of unkempt beauty.

Pedimented estate cottages in mellow brick the colour of dark nasturtiums, the old school and a smithy straddle the wide street which leads to just about the best village green you could wish for. A Gothic Revival pump stands in its midst. On one side of the green between the pantile-roofed houses and cottages, there is a bow-windowed tea shop, a village store-cum-hairdresser and The Earle Arms, which takes its name from Erasmus Earle, the Cromwellian lawyer who bought Heydon Hall in 1650. On the south side of the green is a perfect Miss Mitford residence, cosy village Georgian covered in rose-clad trellis. The lane passes by, leading towards high trees and a hidden rectory. On the north side, a row of tiny gabled cottages is dwarfed by the great flint Perpendicular church behind it.

Inside the church of St Peter and St Paul the arch over the west door is as lofty and lovely as could be. If you look ahead to the top of the fourteenth-century rood screen you will see a white barn owl. Still and stuffed, it is meant to scare bats away. The tub-shaped font is fourteenth-century and there are lots of hatchments, monuments and a mortuary chapel to the Bulwers of Heydon.

Beyond the green, between two gate lodges with swooping Dutch gables, a drive leads across a sylvan park complete with Stubbs-like images of fine shiny horses grazing under oak trees to a direct view of Heydon Hall. A rose-red beauty of an Elizabethan house, it is framed by a wide flank of oak and beech behind yew hedges.

Heydon Hall faces out towards a distant chestnut avenue, ending in a view of Cawston's great church spire. With its three pinnacled gables and clustered chimneys soaring above, the house was built in the 1580s by Henry Dynne, the auditor of the Exchequer, and ended up with the Bulwer family when it passed to Mrs Bulwer, Erasmus Earle's sister.

Around the house and clinging to its east side is a veritable village of mellow-brick buildings – stables, barns, a clock tower, a walled potager. There are orchards and a garden of wide lawns and cedars, secret paths winding away through rhododendrons and mop-head may trees, statues and glimpses of ancient sweet chestnuts in the park beyond.

Right: Heydon's Perpendicular church and the village green

High Force, **County Durham**

High Force could be in South America. Even from afar the muffled thunder of it is awe-inspiring. As you get nearer on the sinuous path, past moss-covered crags to which stalwart beech trees cling with octopus-like roots, past ash saplings sticking to vertical cliffs above the great River Tees, the sound becomes a terrifying roar. Standing below the foaming white water mass which falls from a seventy-foot-high sill into the deep dark pool of burnt umber-coloured river, you expect an Amazonian tribesman to appear from behind a rock at any minute.

In fact it is in County Durham – always a different domain – the land of Prince Bishops and a county palatine set apart from England and Scotland. The mighty River Tyne marks its northern boundary and the Tees spreads its pools and tumbles through the south. At Scotch Corner you can turn westwards and make for Greta Bridge, which spans the river in a simple elegant sweep and was designed in the eighteenth century by John Carr of York for the owners of Rokeby Park. Just beyond is The Morrit Arms, a coaching inn where Dickens really did stay to write *Nicholas Nickleby* and whose bar is covered in murals painted in 1946 by Gilroy, the originator of the Guinness advertisements.

The journey up the valley of the Tees to High Force begins past Rokeby Park, its plain Palladian façade looking straight into the morning sun, reserved and elegant. On up the valley, the spectacular ruins of Egglestone Abbey stand on a plateau high over a deep gorge of the Tees; a few cottages edge the small, sheep-grazed green beside it. The sylvan scene is soon hit for six by the mountainous Bowes Museum – a vast château plucked from the Loire and dropped by the Tees in the nineteenth century. It looks positively startling and houses the most wonderfully eclectic collection of art and artefacts, all thanks to John Bowes, the bastard son of the Earl of Strathmore.

The museum stands on the edge of Barnard Castle, a tip-top market town with wide streets of handsome houses, some of the local pinkish-grey stone, some white-stuccoed with black-painted window surrounds. A beautiful octagonal market cross commands the view down the steep hill called the Bank, and the great Norman ruined castle rises dramatically above the river. Out from the town, the road leads on up verdant Teesdale, which is full of treasures such as spring gentians, bird's-eye primroses, cinquefoils, nine species of lady's mantle and, in the high pastures, 'double dumpling' orchids. On past walled and tree-speckled pastures, through Lartington and ravishing wide-greened villages like Cotherstone and Romaldkirk, you reach Mickleton, set on a slope among sycamores in bigger bolder country. Nearby, the lost railway line is choked with rosebay willowherb and the fields thick with ragwort.

All around, there are farms on the hillsides and a cattle market smelling of disinfectant beside the bridge, which leads across to Middleton in Teesdale, a fine and satisfactory little town with a huge pinnacled Methodist chapel. Proper shops and big beech and sycamore trees line the main street, Horsemarket.

Leaving this, the capital of Upper Teesdale, the country becomes bleaker with outcrops of the dark resistant Whinstone rock which form vertical cliffs, scars and waterfalls. The Cauldron Snout, a spectacular cascade, is hidden in the hills, and near Low Force, Europe's earliest suspension bridge spans the Tees. But it is High Force, the mightiest waterfall in England, which caps all.

Left: High Force waterfall

Holt, **Norfolk**

Norfolk has the least rainfall and the clearest visibility in England, and it is not as flat as is usually supposed. There is a small hill climb as you approach Holt from the south under the broad, bright skies. Sheep are scattered across brown fields of roots, gorse and bracken. Silver birches edge the black pine forests on Edgefield Heath, and amelanchier showers pink blossom on the gardens on the outskirts of one of England's friendliest small towns. Holt is satisfactorily compact, the High Street just the right length, and the playing fields and handsome brick blocks of Gresham's School, founded in 1555 by Sir John Gresham (W H Auden and Benjamin Britten were among its pupils), lend a feeling of settled continuity to the place. To the north, Holt peters out into breckland stretching down to the fresh salt marshes of Cley, Blakeney and the sea.

There is a harmonious feeling about Holt which has something to do with the town having been rebuilt all of a piece in the eighteenth century, following a disastrous fire. Over the course of three hours, the medieval town was razed to the ground and the thatched roof of the Norman church destroyed, leaving its interior in devastation. Today Holt remains remarkably unspoiled and its local building styles and materials tell of nothing but Norfolk. In the market place, the High Street and through all the little side streets, alleys and courtyards, there is a predominance of pantile roofs, colour-wash, pebble and flint and brick houses, some with swooping Dutch gables.

Holt is one of the few towns in the country in which I enjoy shopping. This is because it is the right scale and there are almost no chain shops. Instead there is a good mixture of new independent ones, like the razzle-dazzle François Bouttier's 'studio', where you can buy exotic frocks, or the North Norfolk Fish Company in Old Stable Yard, who sell local oysters, crabs and armfuls of samphire gathered from the salt marshes. A painting of bream by a retired local farmer hangs over the counter. Past Benbows, spilling its fruit, veg, tulips and polyanthus onto the pavement beside the King's Head, is the famous Bakers & Larners, ship's chandlers and ironmongers established in the 1770s, who eventually joined forces to become a small department store. Known as 'the Harrods of the East', the shop meanders in a series of wandering rooms where smiling ladies sell plates painted with sheep and horses, Norfolk lavender bags, crystal glasses, china dogs and chickens, tea cozies in the shape of cottages and cats, electric kettles and toasters, pink umbrellas, camping equipment, Stanley stoves, gold sandals with wedge heels, shopping trolleys, shaving mirrors, silk delphiniums, handbags and bath mats. The food hall has an eight-yard-long set of shelves of floor-to-ceiling chocolates and a counter selling 115 different cheeses, including local Wissington, Wighton and White Lady, all made in Wells-next-the-Sea.

The second-hand bookshop in a higgledy-piggledy house on Fish Hill has a narrow, winding stair leading to half a dozen small book-lined rooms, where the floorboards creek and the low windows give on to a sea of pantiled roofs. Part of the ritual of coming to Holt is to end up on Shirehall Plain under a beamed ceiling in Byfords café. Horace Walpole may have hated the 'wilds of Norfolk', but if he had sat in Byfords and warmed up a little after feeling the cold, biting wind coming off the sea, he might have thought differently.

Left: Shirehall Plain in Holt, one of the friendliest shopping towns in the country

Honington, **Warwickshire**

Down the big bold Cotswold hills, past the Whispering Knights and the Rollright Stones, Warwickshire's less swaggering terrain begins. At Long Compton, where a tiny cottage sits over the church lychgate, the feeling of the Cotswolds fades fast. Stone gives way to bright brick and half-timbering. The plough sweeps in chocolate furrows across the fields and Brailes Hill rises like a hump-backed whale from the mild landscape. Henry James wrote in *English Hours*: 'There is no better way to plunge *in medias res*, for the stranger who wishes to know something of England, than to spend a fortnight in Warwickshire. It is the core and centre of the English world: midmost England, unmitigated England.'

Towards Stratford on the eastern banks of the deep-cut River Stour, the village of Honington lies in uneventful, hedgy meadow country. A pair of elegant gate piers topped with pineapples stands on either side of the road and heralds the way on the public road across a classical four-arched bridge with ball finials on its parapets. From here, between the leaning alders on the river bank and across a sheep-strewn park, you can glimpse Honington Hall, a gem of a Carolean house from whose windows the bridge was designed to be seen. The Hall has an indefinable rightness of scale about it. Only Warwickshire could have produced the rich hues of its building materials: brick the colour of mid-red wallflowers with stone dressings of orangey-gold. Over the ground-floor windows are busts of Roman emperors let into stone arches. Beyond it, an Elizabethan stable arch tells of an earlier house which once stood nearby. The lichen-encrusted church of All Saints is set amidst a graveyard circled with trees. Classical, neat and orderly, masking the thirteenth-century tower tucked up behind, its pale blue interior is light, spacious and divided by Tuscan arcades. The box pews were cut down by the Victorians but an original children's box pew remains at the back of the church. Sir Henry Parker, MP for Evesham, a merchant who owned a coffee house near the Temple and who built the present Hall in 1682, is depicted in white-veined marble in an elaborate monument to his memory on the west wall. In his high-heeled buckled shoes and voluminous cloak, and with his long curly wig hanging halfway down his back, he looks self-important as he walks with his son, Hugh, who predeceased him.

A walled drive overhung with yews leads away from the church into the golden-stoned village. The main street is set with wide grass verges and an avenue of young chestnut trees. Houses and cottages are generously spaced on either side and a second set of elaborately grand gate piers rise imperiously, trumpeting another entrance to the Hall. Beyond them a view spreads to the far-off and lofty spire of Tredington church. Magpie House, half-timbered with zigzag diagonal bracing and looking suitably Shakespearean, commands the village street from one end, and further on there is a diamond-window-paned, marmalade-stone cottage, its front garden edged with pinks, valerian and rose-coloured hydrangeas, and its front door guarded by perfectly sculpted topiary snail shells of box. A satisfactory brick farmhouse, ivy neatly trimmed against it, stands across the road, but the star of the show in this kempt, neat-as-a-pin village is at the eastern end. Rose Cottage, small and thatched, pale blue paintwork against its whitewashed walls, pink roses and lavender beyond the picket gate, is as pretty as could be. Though Henry James was surely in love with the mystique of the English country house, 'in such a region as this mellow conservative Warwickshire,' he wrote, 'an appreciative American finds the small things just as appreciative as the great.'

Right: Rose Cottage
Inset: Honington Hall

Right: John Piper's stained-glass window in Iffley Church
Inset: the elaborate Norman carving around the west door

Iffley, Oxford

A couple of miles from the middle of Oxford, on a low hill above water meadows and the wandering Thames, the village of Iffley remains one of my favourite places of all. If you were thundering around Oxford on the southern bypass you wouldn't notice it was there, half-hidden as it is in trees. But if you have a moment to spare, head towards Oxford on the Iffley Road, between the interminable rows of villas which have swamped the fields, and turn off down Church Way. Within a minute you are in another world. Like a phoenix rising from the acres of suburban sprawl, the old limestone village begins to unfurl along the lane. A completely different atmosphere pervades. You feel settled and at peace again. There are thatched cottages and viburnum bushes billowing from behind garden walls. The plaque on the little stucco house at 103 Church Way reads, 'Mrs Sarah Nowell's School 1822'. The vicar of Iffley's wife left an endowment in her will to build a larger and handsome thatched school further up the road, which now acts as the church hall. A small lane trickles down past the gabled rectory to a distant view of Oxford's gleaming spires, while ahead an enormous horse chestnut spreads its generous shade over the church gate. More chestnuts surround the churchyard, and beyond the land falls sharply away to the Thames which splits into two and forms a long lozenge-shaped island. On the eastern bank are the ruins of Iffley Mill, built in the eleventh century, which survived until it was destroyed by fire in 1908.

Iffley Church is magnificent. Stalwart, strong and Romanesque, it was built all of a piece in the twelfth century with Iffley quarry stone. The St Remy family owned the place at the time and were probably responsible. The Norman carving on the window- and door-surrounds is breathtaking – great zigzag and beakhead arches interspersed with monsters, signs of the zodiac and fighting horsemen. Inside, the mighty Romanesque arches are just as good, but it is the south-west window which draws your gaze. Designed by John Piper, it was given to the church by his widow Myfanwy as a memorial to him in 1995. It is in bright rich colours on an electric-blue ground and depicts a tree of life with birds and animals, echoing the Romanesque style which Piper loved so much.

Sadly nothing remains of Annora's cell, which used to be attached to the church. She was the resident anchoress (a holy hermit) soon after the church was built. King John had a blazing row with her father, William de Braose, and proceeded to persecute the whole family, starving two of them to death. Annora ended up living in the tiny cell for nine years. The blocked-up arch in the east end of the church might have been part of a window through which she could have seen the altar. Henry III, King John's son, felt so ashamed of his father's cruelty to her family that he plied Annora with gifts of grain, clothing and timber from his forests.

Best of all would be to approach Iffley by boat and walk up the steep path to the village. The Second World War poet Keith Douglas wrote to his sweetheart:

Whistle and I will hear
and come another evening, when this boat
travels with you alone towards Iffley:
as you lie looking up for thunder again,
this cool touch does not betoken rain;
it is my spirit that kisses your mouth lightly.

Douglas was killed in Normandy at the age of twenty-four.

Ightham Mote, **Kent**

With its lush gardens and thick fern-filled woods, Kent must be the cosiest county in England. It has chalk downs, oast-houses, blood-red splashes of poppies across small cornfields, tile-hung and clapboarded houses and cottages, Kentish ragstone churches with hunched wooden bell-towers, steep deep lanes dipping down into shaded dells, and place names that often end in '-den' (Horsmonden, Tenterden, Smarden) meaning wooded glade or a forest retreat.

The village of Ightham is full of comforting half-timbering and the medieval church contains some beautiful monuments, mostly to the Selby family. Dorothy Selby, who died in 1641, was famous for her needlework and is said to have deciphered a coded message which led to the discovery of the Gunpowder Plot. Her memorial describes how her 'curious needle turned th'abused stage / Of this lewd world into a Golden Age'.

Nearby, in a wooded cleft of the Kentish Weald, the lane leads down under a dark tunnel of nut trees to the Selby family home of Ightham Mote, one of the loveliest medieval and Tudor manor-houses in England. This is E Nesbit country where, as a child, she came to live for three happy years. Her children's books, from *Five Children and It* to *The Railway Children*, are laced with descriptions of Kent, and Ightham Mote recalls Albert's uncle's house in *The Wouldbegoods*:

'The Moat House was the one we went to stay at. There has been a house there since Saxon times. It is a manor, and a manor goes on having a house on it whatever happens. The Moat House was burnt down once or twice in ancient centuries – I don't remember which – but they always built a new one, and Cromwell's soldiers smashed it about, but it was patched again... The doors were locked. There were green curtains, and honeycomb for breakfast. After brekker my father went back to town, and Albert's uncle went too, to see publishers. We saw them to the station, and Father gave us a long list of what we weren't to do...'

To arrive at Ightham Mote on a sunny afternoon during the week (there are busloads of visitors on Sundays) is to walk straight into a safe-feeling E Nesbit story – you know there is bound to be a happy ending. There are ducks on the moat, pink valerian clinging to the brick and stonework, leaded lights, half-timbering in box-frames of silvery oak. It would be hard to find anywhere more romantic. It is the sort of place you would like to linger in indefinitely. There is a feeling of peace in its enclosure which is almost tangible. Inside the house there are seventy-three higgledy-piggledy rooms of different dates and heights and on different levels encircling the courtyard – an oriel room, a solar, chapels, a crypt, an apple store, halls, boys' room, drawing-room, billiards-room and butler's pantry. From the 1300s onwards Cawnes, Hauts, Clements, Allens and Selbys lived here until the end of the nineteenth century when Sir Thomas Colyer-Fergusson bought it. His grandson, Sir James, eventually sold it to an American bachelor called Charles Henry Robinson who came from Portland in Maine and who fell for the house, hook, line and sinker. He lavished love and money on it for the next thirty-odd years and left it to the National Trust.

A stream meanders through the garden and falls into the moat. According to the *Gardeners' Chronicle* of 2nd February 1889, 'lazy young gentlemen have been known to lay on their couches and fish out of the window... Ferns revel in the shady nooks, and the whole has a beautiful gardenesque but at the same time quaint old-world look, which is perfectly delightful.'

Right: Ightham Mote, a moated medieval manor-house
Inset: detail of the old manor-house

Kelmscott Manor, **Gloucestershire**

It isn't hard to imagine William Morris arriving by boat through the winding upper reaches of the Thames with his friend Dante Gabriel Rossetti and seeing this house for the first time. 'Through the hawthorn sprays and long shoots of the wild roses,' he wrote, 'I could see the flat country spreading out far away under the sea of the calm evening, till something that might be called hills, with a look of sheep pastures about them, bounded it with a soft blue line. Before me, the elm boughs still hid most of what houses there might be in this river-side dwelling of men; but to the right of the cart-road a few grey buildings of the simplest kind showed here and there... We crossed the road, and again, almost without my will, my hand raised to the latch of a door, and we stood presently on a stone path which led up to the old house.'

Kelmscott Manor is well hidden. The peaceful village lies across willowy meadowland approached by dog-legged lanes or a short track up from the river mooring. The houses and cottages are built in the same local pale-golden limestone as the 'manor', an unassuming sixteenth-century farmhouse. It was built by the Turner family, who farmed the surrounding land for three centuries, adding a wing in the 1670s. In 1871 they let it to William Morris and Dante Gabriel Rossetti, who had fallen in love with it. As you wind down the narrow lane, past The Plough Inn, the glorious gabled manor, glimpsed first above the secretive garden wall, does not flaunt itself. Its façade is just as it was when Charles Gere drew it in 1892 for the frontispiece of *News from Nowhere*, William Morris's periodical published by his own Kelmscott Press. The inside of the house is much as it was in the 1870s when Morris, the craftsman, poet, manufacturer and socialist, was designing the 'Willow Bough' wallpaper, writing *The Haystack in the Floods*, and watching his wife Jane fall in love with Rossetti. The atmosphere is still filled with these three Pre-Raphaelites, their friends and generations of Turners before them. The furnishings are hand-woven, the furniture hand-hewn. The sixteenth-century part of the house is rambling and small-roomed; the seventeenth-century addition is more open and elegant with Renaissance fireplaces and Georgian panelling.

Everywhere you look there are paintings by Rossetti, tiles by William De Morgan, embroidered curtains by Jane, wall-hangings by Morris and richly decorated Kelmscott Press books. It does not feel in the least like a museum. When you look from a bedroom window you can see the River Thames meandering down from Lechlade towards Oxford. The border encircling the top of the four-poster bed is hung with Morris's words, embroidered by his daughter May: 'The wind's on the wold / And the night is a-cold / And Thames runs chill / 'Twixt mead and hill / But kind and dear / Is the old house here / And my heart is warm / Midst winter's harm.'

Kelmscott Manor is a hard place to leave. Its peace is overwhelming. Morris died in the early autumn of 1896 and was carried through the village in a yellow farm wagon with red wheels wreathed with vine and willow boughs. Following the same route today, you pass the cottage Ernest Gimson designed for May Morris in 1915, and the William Morris memorial cottages designed by his close friend Philip Webb for Jane in 1902. On the outside wall there is a stone relief of William Morris carved from a sketch by Webb. The village hall was also designed by Ernest Gimson. Last of all, in the small churchyard of St George, hidden behind a large bay tree, is the grave of William Morris, marked by Webb's plain coped stone and carved with the simplest lettering. Jane, Jenny and May lie beside him.

Far left: Kelmscott Manor
Inset: the frontispiece from *News from Nowhere* shows the east front of Kelmscott, drawn by Charles Gere

Kensal Green Cemetery, **London**

Late winter is the season to stoke up the spirit of melancholy. Winding up the river-like Harrow Road towards Wembley, or stepping out from Kensal Green Underground station, where the gasworks fill half the south-west sky and the shop windows of monumental masons flaunt polished granite headstones and grave dressings of bright purple gravel, you will find a stately Greek triumphal arch heralding the most romantic necropolis in town. Here, in this strange paradise, deserted paths lead endlessly this way and that under great lime trees and evergreen oaks. All around lie thousands of late Londoners under tombstones tipping this way and that, or under ever-grander Victorian stone canopies, obelisks, sarcophagi, draped urns and sphinxes. Some are swamped in over a century's tangled ivy while others, more recent, are piled high with artificial flowers. A robin perches on an angel's fingers and you can often be completely alone here in seventy acres of beauty.

Life falls quietly into perspective. Humility and awe take over. Here lies the author of *The Woman in White*, Wilkie Collins, side by side with his mistress. Here too are Trollope, Thackeray and Blondin, the most famous tightrope-walker of all time, who crossed the Niagara Falls in 1859 on a high wire. Here is 'Boots' Davidson, who introduced the Trinidad steel band to Britain and whose dancing funeral procession in 1933 was attended by thousands. Here are Dr James Barry, the pioneering woman doctor who became the General of the Army Medical Department in the guise of a man; George Grossmith, joint author with his brother Weedon of *The Diary of a Nobody*; Thomas Hood, who wrote 'The Song of the Shirt', and, being always in debt, mortgaged his brain in exchange for a cash advance. A monument to the illustrator George Cruikshank, a reformed alcoholic, proclaims him a champion of 'universal abstinence from intoxicating drinks'. Nearby lie the young men who never heeded him: Viscount Strangford, a dazzling, handsome rake who died from brandy, dissipation and consumption, and Viscount Hastings, the 'King of Plungers', who eloped with Sir Henry Chaplin's fiancée and ruined himself by gambling. He died in 1868.

The Grand Union Canal runs silently along the southern boundary of the cemetery. Beyond it, Isambard Kingdom Brunel's Great Western Railway begins one of the most brilliant journeys of all time, tunnelled and viaducted to Penzance. Within earshot of the clattering track lies the great engineer himself, alongside his father, under a simple block of Portland stone.

Perhaps the grandest and most elaborate monument of all, in complete contrast, is a huge Greco-Egyptian mausoleum, guarded by sphinxes and decorated with beehives, horses, angels, shells, glass balls and foliage. It was built by the famous circus-performer Andrew Ducrow (1793–1842), the colossus of equestrians, for his wife, a lady rider. He is buried here too, his gloves and ringmaster's hat carved in stone.

Conceived in the 1820s, Kensal Green Cemetery was the first to be established beyond the limits of the metropolis, in what was then open country. The General Cemetery Company was formed, and by mid-1833 received its first funeral. By the end of the century the company could proudly claim some royal dukes and five hundred members of the titled nobility lying beneath its turf. The same company still runs it to this day. As one of the world's first garden cemeteries, it was designed in the spirit of an English country park and the landscaping and planting were much influenced by John Claudius Loudon, the famous gardener who is also buried here. The Victorian cemetery ideal was that they should be 'sweet breathing places', set aside for contemplative recreation, spiritual enlightenment and general education of the living. Nothing has changed.

Left: Kensal Green cemetery in winter
Below: detail of the cemetery in spring

Kimmeridge to Kingston, Dorset

I left the thatched village of Kimmeridge and strange slatey ledges of the horseshoe-shaped bay hundreds of feet below. A low tide had exposed a mass of bladderack seaweed in the shallows, and from these high hills the fossil hunters combing the jagged seascape looked like ants.

There is pink thrift carpeting the short-cropped turf, and the lonely folly, built by the Reverend Clavell in 1830 as an observatory, stands anew, moved lock stock and barrel to safer ground, well back from the eroding cliff's edge. Walking east along the bold saddle of the Purbeck Hills towards Kingston, the outline of St Alban's Head is just visible jutting out into the Channel through the heat haze shimmering off the sea.

These voluptuous chalk uplands above the Jurassic coast, rising and falling in gigantic waves all around, are perhaps the most noble in England. Inland to the north a deep valley falls away, harbouring raggle-taggle farms, secret cottages, small woods and prehistoric settlements. Halfway up the slope on the opposite side, the pretty limestone village of Church Knowle is clustered around the church with the ancient Barneston Manor nearby.

Half smothered in brambles, a silvery dry-stone wall snakes beside the path, and patches of gorse cling to the hillside facing the sea. A young man with a scarlet paraglider stands on the steep slope ahead and then suddenly runs off the edge, lifted on a pocket of wind. Now he glides like a seagull catching the breezes. Below him Smedmore House lies safely sheltered from gales by trees on the small table of land above the cliffs.

The path leads on to Swyre Head from where a bigger view than ever spreads out to infinity. On a clear day you can see Dartmoor to the west, and to the east the Isle of Wight and the Needles. Whoever is buried in the barrow on Swyre Head's summit chose a prime spot. These hills, from which you could easily spot the enemy approaching from any direction, have always been strategically important and are scattered with Iron Age, Roman and Saxon remains.

Beyond a great oak wood whose wind-blown trees are bent like old men away from the sea, there are patches of bright blue squill in the turf and hundreds of sheep scattered down the hillside. An obelisk like Cleopatra's Needle strikes up into the sky ahead. It was erected to commemorate a member of the Scott family whose eighteenth-century pile, built of the palest lichen-covered Portland stone, is tantalisingly obscured by trees in the natural amphitheatre below. The writer David Cecil, on approaching Encombe House down a long winding wooded drive in the 1980s, wrote: 'The site of a building so grand but hidden away in remote woodland at the brink of the ocean stirred my emotion to conjure up all sorts of romantic fancies about its history and its inhabitants.'

The Scotts, who became Earls of Eldon, had grand ideas. In the kempt estate village of Kingston, high on its windy ridge, their Victorian pride and piety knew no bounds. The arch-reactionary Lord Chancellor Eldon rebuilt the old church in 1838, and in 1873 his twenty-eight-year-old descendant commissioned another in the form of a miniature cathedral, whose tower can be seen from half of Dorset. He insisted on using local materials and craftsmen and it cost him £70,000 to build over a period of seven years. The church's architect, G E Street, who was justly proud of it and of all the scores he had built, called it his 'jolliest church'. It is not what you expect to find in a small Dorset village – 'Gothic architecture at its most classical and least quirky,' Alec Clifton Taylor wrote. 'If it is chilly it is the chilliness of perfection.' From the garden of The Scott Arms, the view across the mist-hung valley to Corfe Castle on its mound, with Poole harbour beyond, is ethereal. It is like an illustration for a medieval fairy story.

Left: the view from Swyre Head overlooking Kimmeridge Bay with Weymouth in the distance

105

Leighton Hall, **Lancashire**

Not far from Carnforth Station, where *Brief Encounter* was filmed, the road up Peter Hill from Yealand Conyers winds between outcrops of silvery stone. It climbs almost vertically until, at the very top, a modest lodge and gateposts herald the first glorious view of Leighton Hall. The house lies halfway down a great wide sweep of Utopian parkland, laid out in 1763. The whole scene is like a painting of some fantastic, imaginary landscape. Over to the west, a mile or two away across wooded hills, the sea sparkles in Morecambe Bay. Behind the house, the mountainous lakeland hills and rocky cliffs rise in a distant and majestic backdrop, while down at the bottom of the valley lies Leighton Moss, a huge marshy mere, the home of a quarter of Britain's bittern population. It is the largest remaining reedbed in north-west England and is the haunt of a host of bearded tits and marsh harriers.

The facade of Leighton Hall, all pale shimmering limestone quarried from nearby, is in the neo-Gothic style of the early nineteenth century, while somewhere behind it are the vestiges of a Georgian house built around Tudor and Jacobean ruins. The Gillow family of Lancaster, renowned cabinet-makers and staunch Roman Catholics all, are inextricably woven into Leighton Hall's history, and Gillow descendants still live here.

As a ship's carpenter in the West Indies, Robert Gillow had brought back the first shipment of mahogany to England in the 1730s, and together with his sons proceeded to create some of the finest furniture ever made. Fifty years on, Gillows was the biggest furniture company in Europe, and in 1810 the firm's accountant performed, in effect, a management buy-out from the three Gillow brothers, Robert, George and Richard, the grandsons of the founder. Free from a full-time commitment to the firm, the three brothers, with their good Catholic pedigrees and their enormous bank balances, were ripe fodder for the impoverished Catholic aristocracy, and they all proceeded to marry grand women.

Richard, who bought Leighton Hall in 1822, married a Miss Stapleton from Carlton Towers in Yorkshire. Together they added the fashionable Gothic façade to Leighton as well as extra rooms to accommodate the fourteen children they produced. In the hall they made a delicate curving cantilevered staircase, and everywhere they set down elegant Gillow furniture. Today the famous 'daisy table' stands in the hall with its eight petalled edges which turn down on individual flaps. There is also a Gillow games table, a satin writing table and a lady's workbox made especially for Mrs Richard Gillow in 1825.

Richard's eldest son, also Richard, lived until he was ninety-nine and was known as 'Old Squire'. He drained some of Leighton Moss and made it into cornfields, and commissioned the well-known firm of Austin and Paley of Lancaster to build on a fitting Gothic wing to the Hall in which to house a billiard-room. (This later became a music-room where the great opera singer, Kathleen Ferrier, gave her last performance.) 'Old Squire' also got Mr Paley to build a new Roman Catholic church in Yealand Conyers, affirming the long-standing Gillow faith in a village which was famously associated with the persecution of the Quaker movement. In the mid-seventeenth century, the Quaker leader, George Fox, preached here and was supported by Richard Hubberstone, a local man who proved particularly invaluable in organising secret Quaker meetings in the area. He continued to uphold the faith until he died in Newgate Prison. For many visitors to Yealand, the object of their journey is to visit the '1652 country' where, in that year, the Society of Friends was established. The Yealand Meeting House, built in 1692 as a result of George Fox's visits, is still in use, as is the burial ground.

Right: Leighton Hall near Carnforth

Liberty, London

Few department stores in London retain their original character. Most have been homogenised and swished up beyond recognition. John Lewis, for instance, has become a gleaming, futuristic space full of elevators carrying scores of worried-looking shoppers. Whitley's has long been a shopping mall, chopped and changed and filled with ubiquitous shops (though at least the long-fought campaign to retain the glorious double-flighted staircase was won). Marshall & Snellgrove – the setting for the most dramatic Victorian elopement when the Pocket Venus dived through its front doors on the pretext of buying something, ran through to the back of the shop and into the arms of the rake Lord Hastings, who whisked her away in his carriage – is no longer. Peter Jones has had a radical facelift, Fenwick feels like a store in New York, Harrods was always too big for me to handle, but Liberty – ah, Liberty. Its comfort and succour are always there. It has hardly changed and its founder's intuitive vision and pioneering spirit are ever-present.

The son of a draper, Arthur Lasenby Liberty was born in Chesham in 1843. He did his apprenticeship with a firm of drapers in Baker Street and was first employed by Farmer and Roger's Shawl and Cloak Emporium in 1862. It was the year of the International Exhibition at Kensington and this made such an impression on Arthur that he began to harbour dreams of having a shop of his own; he believed that he could change the look of homeware and fashion. A dozen years later, with a loan of £1,500 from his future father-in-law, Arthur bought the lease of 218a Regent Street. His shop opened in 1875, selling ornaments, fabric and objets d'art, and within eighteen months he had repaid his loan and acquired the second half of 218. As the business grew he added on neighbouring properties, which accounts for the quirky layout of the store.

Few people can claim to have been so influential in the history of modern design as Arthur Liberty. Although originally importing things from Japan and the East, he fast became the commissioner of some of the finest British avant-garde designers of the time. Leading Pre-Raphaelite, Arts and Crafts and Art Nouveau movers and shakers, who believed in all aspects of the arts, were involved and contributed to Liberty's products with innovative homeware, furniture, pottery and even clothes. A costume department was opened under the directorship of the distinguished architect Edward Godwin, and Archibald Knox designed metal-wear, jewellery, garden ornaments and carpets. It seemed a natural step to open a second store in Birmingham – a hub of the Arts and Crafts movement and home of Morris and Co.

Arthur commissioned Edwin T Hall and his son Edwin to design the familiar and homely mock-Tudor building in London. It was built using the timbers of two ships: HMS *Impregnable* and HMS *Hindustan* (the frontage on Great Marlborough Street is the same length as the Hindustan). Sadly Arthur did not live to see its completion, but his wishes were fulfilled. He had always insisted on his store feeling homely and intimate. Many of the rooms had fireplaces, some of which still exist. The wells created opportunities for draping rugs and fabric and the smaller rooms were perfect for selling smaller things. Arthur's ghost is still there today, and to travel in a panelled lift to the needlework department is comforting beyond compare.

Left: the mock-Tudor façade of Liberty on Great Marlborough Street

Linton-in-Craven and Thorpe-sub-Montem, **Yorkshire**

In high Wharfedale, little changes but for the gradual carving out of the banks by the river Wharfe which hurries on through shallow brown pools and over its bouldered bottom. Turner painted here while Ruskin mused, 'Throughout the dale there floats a feeling of this mountain power, and an instinctive apprehension of the strength and greatness of the wild northern land.' Certainly I am fearful of 'the Strid', where the river narrows between mossy rocks into a ten-foot-wide gorge of fierce white water roaring into a thirty-foot-deep cauldron below.

Past the village of Burnsall, settled into a tree-sprinkled bowl of the hills, the dale widens out, crisscrossed with myriad stone walls. A tiny lane leads off towards the looming Raven Nest Crags, Kail Hill and Elbolton Hill where, a hundred years ago in a cave below the summit, the remains of bears, wolves, boars and humans were found. The lane loops down between silvery walls of large rounded stones stacked above eye level. No lorry could ever squeeze through to the tiny lost hamlet of Thorpe-in-the-Hollow, as it is sometimes called, enveloped in these cushions of hills. It feels as utterly secret today as it did when it was used for hiding stock and dalesmen from marauders. Thorpe has long been known as the 'hidden hamlet', for it escaped the depredations of the fourteenth-century Scottish raiders who passed down the dale, missing it completely.

Round the last bend you come upon the handsomest classical eighteenth-century farmhouse imaginable, roses stuffed into its front garden and with raggle-taggle barns and farm buildings around it. Two chained-up sheep dogs wag their tails outside their tin-barrel kennels, a broken-down David Brown tractor waits to be mended on the verge and two clipped lollipop holly trees stand sentinel either side of a cottage gate, as high as the roof. The people of Thorpe were famous shoemakers and supplied the monks at Fountains Abbey. Until fifty years ago a shoemaker lived in a cottage on the lane which peters out into a track and a moorland path; the second lane leads to Threapland and Cracoe; the third back onto the road for Linton.

Linton is a different cup of tea altogether, set in a wide open stretch of land a little further up the dale. There was once a lake here and the people of Linton grew flax around it, from which they made linen – hence its name. Stone houses and cottages are spread around a generous and irregularly shaped green through which the Eller Beck flows. Thirty brown ducks and one white one waddle around in a busy group. A clapper bridge, a packhorse bridge and stepping stones cross this way and that under tall beech trees and sycamores. There is a manor-house and farm, two rectories, a post office, a yeoman's house and a pub called The Black Sheep. It is a loved village, but without a hint of self-conscious conservation about it – it is not tarted up or over-restored or twee, but reserved and unflashy.

Except, that is, for the grandest set of almshouses in all England which dominate one side of the green. They were founded by Richard Fountaine, who was born in Linton in 1639 and became a London timber merchant during the Plague and the Fire of London, when timber was in great demand. He made a fortune, and when he died at the age of eighty-one he left money for a mini Castle Howard to be built of millstone grit from Thorpe Fell. It provides six cottages and a chapel in the centre. There is ongoing debate as to whether the architect Vanbrugh designed the building or not: he designed an identical set of almshouses for his parish in London but they were never built. He also used Fountaine as his timber merchant.

Left: Richard Fountaine's almshouses in Linton

Little Gidding, Cambridgeshire

The tiny church of St John the Evangelist at Little Gidding is in obscure and isolated country where flattish watery pastures, wide-verged lanes and distant pylons abound. Farms stand on mild rises. To a small hill above the Alconbury Brook, set between Steeple and Great Gidding, up a long-lost avenue of trees, Nicholas Ferrar made his way in the early 1620s. Here he found the decaying moated manor-house of Little Gidding and the abandoned parish church – its nave a barn, its vestry a pigsty. The place was, 'with respect to privacy of situation, exactly suited to his wishes.' His strength of purpose and the small community he founded here, though it lasted only twenty-five years, remain an inspiration to this day. Little Gidding soon became a place of pilgrimage and a muse to T S Eliot:

There are other places
Which also are the world's end, some at the sea jaws,
Or over a dark lake, in a desert or a city –
But this is the nearest, in place and time,
Now and in England.

Nicholas Ferrar was born in London in 1592, the son of a founder of the Virginia Company. His rapid grasp of Greek and Latin enabled him to go to Clare College, Cambridge, at the age of fourteen, and he later studied abroad and became the perfect Renaissance man – a fine scholar, a natural leader and a powerful speaker. He set himself the highest standards and his qualities were well known at the court of King James. However, he grew increasingly depressed by the world he saw around him. Although he served in Parliament for a brief period, he was saddened by the lack of principles and blatant debauchery and corruption in royal and political circles, and by 1624 had taken the decision to retire from public life and form a religious community.

The village of Little Gidding, to which Nicholas and his mother retreated, had been victim to the Black Death. There were a few shepherds' cottages and the remains of more. Today the field along which you travel towards the church is probably much as it was then, a series of undulations delineating field systems and the vestiges of a medieval community. The Ferrars put the manor and church in order, and in 1626 Nicholas, who had always had mystical leanings, fasted for eight weeks, after which he was ordained a deacon. A new way of life began at Little Gidding. With the arrival of Nicholas's brother and his wife, children, relations and tutors, the group grew to about forty. They had three services a day and were in close contact with the poet George Herbert, who lived at the neighbouring village of Leighton Bromswold. The women of the group made the most exquisite and now world-famous embroidery, known as 'Opus Little Gidding'. They made covers for the pulpit, reading desk, communion table, kneelers and devotional books – blue for Sundays, green for weekdays. Nicholas believed, like Laud, in expressing the 'beauty of holiness' through decorating the church with fine things – the antithesis of the Puritan movement. King Charles I, a High Anglican married to a Catholic, became very attached to the Ferrar community and its works and often visited Little Gidding – for the last time in 1642, only months before the outbreak of civil war.

Nicholas Ferrar died in 1637, but the community continued until it was pillaged and sacked by the Puritans in 1646, the woodwork burnt, the silver claws from the brass eagle lectern gouged out and the rest chucked into the village pond. Nicholas's nephew John renovated the church in 1714, adding the strange stone facade, remaking the panelling and choir stalls and rescuing the brass font and lectern from the mud, all in memory of his visionary uncle. Today a recently created community has built a pathway and wall of unrelenting red brick which jars, but the church itself remains inspirational.

So, while the light fails
On a winter's afternoon, in a secluded chapel
History is now and England.

Left: St John the Evangelist Church, Little Gidding

Liverpool Cathedral, **Merseyside**

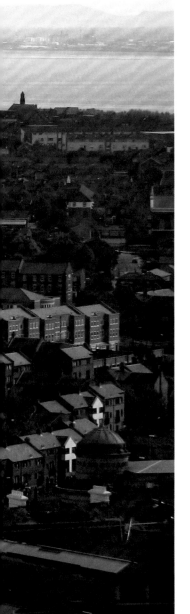

I am in awe of Liverpool. It is a lion-hearted city. Its waterfront and docks along the River Mersey stretch for almost seven miles and the atmosphere of power and strength is overwhelming. Nor do the Liverpool poets exaggerate its romance.

The daughters of Albion
Arriving by underground at Central Station
Eating hot Eccles cakes at the Pierhead
Writing 'Billy Blake is fab' on a wall in Mathew St...

Adrian Henri eulogises the urban idyll and sees the sweet papers in the streets and the rubbish stuck in suburban privet hedges as welcome evidence of human life.

Raw Liverpool does not appeal to everyone – the boarded-up corner shops, the condemned Victorian and Edwardian streets, the weed-filled wastegrounds and cut-price furniture stores – but as Margaret Drabble points out, 'Liverpool is the kind of city which people have to assemble for themselves from unpromising materials – a collage city, for those who can love what is there, rather than yearn for what is gone.'

The pride has certainly not gone and old monuments merely kindle the fire. Perhaps the greatest Victorian monument to civic pride in Britain, St George's Hall, still sails its sixty-foot-high Corinthian columns above the teeming traffic by Lime Street Station. On the waterfront too, bold as brass, are Liverpool's vainglorious symbols of Edwardian prosperity – the Royal Liver Building, the Dock Board Offices and the Cunard Building. But surely the greatest celebration of the Liverpudlian spirit and the supreme testimony of the faith and determination of a community which was never deflected, not even by two world wars, is Liverpool Cathedral. The building began to rise in 1904 when times were brilliant and wasn't completed until 1978 when they were not.

Today the Cathedral soars over the city on St James's Mount – eighteenth-century Liverpool clustered nearby, and beyond the broad sweep down to the dockside are warehouses and commercial monoliths. It is the largest Anglican church in the world and the second largest cathedral after St Peter's in Rome. It is my favourite British cathedral. The sixteenth Earl of Derby, whose family seat is on the outskirts of the city, chaired the original meeting in Liverpool Town Hall in 1901, which marked the start of the realisation of a dream. A national competition was then set up and the twenty-two-year-old Roman Catholic, Giles Gilbert Scott, one of a hundred entrants, submitted the winning design. From then on, Bishop F J Chavasse, the second Bishop of Liverpool, was the leader of the project. 'It must be a cathedral of the people,' he said, 'built by them, thronged by them; their pride, their glory, their spiritual home.' All three men are buried here.

The Cathedral stands beside an abandoned quarry, dramatically deep and wooded, with a graveyard in its depths. It is built of local Woolton sandstone – a sort of dark pinkish colour which resembles milk chocolate in some lights and still looks crisp and pristine despite the city's salty, sooty atmosphere. Over the entrance is Elisabeth Frink's moving sculpture of Christ on the Cross.

Once through the doors of the Cathedral, the scale is awe-inspiring, the vastness and strength of it sublime. 'Don't look at my arches,' said Scott. 'Look at my spaces.' Everything is plain, dignified and gigantic. The height at the undertower is about the same as Nelson's Column and the Gothic arches are purported to be the largest ever built. There can be few greater enclosed spaces in the world. This is a monument and a half – but then nothing in Liverpool is done in half measures.

'Then down the hill,' writes Henri, 'the sound of trumpets / Cheering and shouting in the distance / Children running / Ice-cream vans.'

Left: Liverpool Cathedral

Louth, Lincolnshire

'Those who think of Lincs as dull and flat are wrong,' said my dad. He commissioned his friend Henry Thorold, one of the country's last squarsons, to write the Shell Guide to Lincolnshire. Thorold described Lincolnshire as 'the second largest county in England and the least appreciated' but, he told me, 'the book sold better than every other Shell Guide, except perhaps Cornwall, not because it was a good book but because nobody else had written about this dim county. When people ask me where I live and I say "Lincolnshire", they say, "I don't know the county at all…"' Lincolnshire is certainly maligned and unloved by those who do not know it.

I was lucky enough to travel with Henry Thorold on minor roads through villages with strange names like Boothby Graffoe, whose pubs advertise Bateman's Good Honest Ales, one of the few independent breweries still left in family ownership.

From the Cliff, a long undulating limestone ridge high above the vale, with Lincoln's cathedral rising in the distance like Mont-Saint-Michel from the beach, we crossed the heath, once a wild and desolate place. A lighthouse one hundred and fifty feet high used to guide people across it. On we go down over Blankney Fen beside the great ditch of Timberland Delph to Kirkstead with its ruined abbey and tiny Early English church of St Leonard's.

Next, sandy Scots-piney Woodhall Spa, the golfers' mecca, unfurls its red-brick and half-timbered Edwardian streets which lead to the strange 1920s Kinema-in–the-Woods (Britain's only rear-projection cinema, opened in 1922 and still in use today) and past the mountainous mock-Tudor golfing hotel, and then peters out among gorse bushes towards the foothills of the Wolds. The Wolds are empty. Old drove roads with wide verges climb up into great sweeping countryside. The chalk shows white through the plough on distant curves of land and there are clumps of beech trees along the tops. Suddenly and dramatically Louth church spire cuts into the sky between a gentle fold of hills.

You can enter Louth through Eastgate, Northgate, Westgate, Upgate, Walkergate, Ludgate, Ramsgate, Kidgate, Gospelgate, Cisterngate, or Chequergate. You can vary the pronunciation of its name from 'Louth', which rhymes with 'Mouth', to the two-syllabled version which the locals use – 'Lou-' (like 'cow') '-ath' – or the long-drawn-out one-syllabled version which the old-fashioned gentry use – 'Lou…the'. Whichever way, Louth ranks among my top market towns in England, along with Ludlow, Stamford, Barnard Castle and Devizes. Past Thorpe Hall, an Elizabethan house with tall clustered chimneys haunted by the 'Green Lady', you curl into Westgate and into Louth proper. A rose-red town of more shades of beautiful brick and pantiles than you can ever imagine. Some whitewashed houses are mixed between. The brick runs from the palest apricot through to the richest crimson, the houses from the grandest William and Mary mansion behind high walls to the neatest Georgian doctor's house behind well-clipped laurel hedges. Secret gardens run down to the River Lud, which threads its way through the town from east to west. Louth became a major trading place through the building of its canal in the 1770s, and much of the town is still as Alfred and his brother Charles Tennyson would have known it when they attended Louth Grammar School. From its grass clearing amidst the winding streets, St James's Church rises triumphantly, its spire soaring nearly three hundred feet into the sky – arguably the most beautiful late-Gothic steeple in the country. The mountainous Victorian town hall is described by Thorold as like 'the Vatican in front and a slaughter house behind'. You can enter the covered market nearby under a gaunt Bavarian tower. In a tall house on the market square the bookshop and printers of the two brothers, J and J Jackson, were housed. They printed and published the Tennyson boys' first volume of poems in 1827 and paid them £20.

Louth is still full of proper independent shops: there are six butchers, two grocers, a tailor's and a cobbler's. Unlike so many English towns, which have lost their identities through predictable uniformity, Louth has kept its dignity – and, luckily for it, its distance.

Right: the market town of Louth in Lincolnshire

The Lune Valley,
Lancashire

From Kirkby Lonsdale downstream to Halton, the Lune Valley is undiluted Lancashire – its soil rich and dark, its grass and woodland somehow lusher and a more vivid green than anywhere else. Although the neighbouring Lake District is awash with tourists during the summer months, the Lune Valley remains relatively quiet and off the beaten track, particularly on its northern banks.

Peter Fleetwood-Hesketh, born and bred in the county, wrote of Lancastrians in his *Murray's Architectural Guide*: 'Fundamentally a mixture of Celtic, English, Norse and Dane, they are enterprising and independent and kind, and though their opinions have often been sharply divided … most Lancastrians have a transcending loyalty to their county and one another, a sense of traditions as lively as their sense of humour.' Before it became the County Palatine of Lancaster, Lancashire was the home of the Brigantes, a Celtic confederation of tribes whose lives revolved predominately around agricultural life. In the Lune Valley, the tribes lived peaceably and autonomously in small hamlets of round wooden houses with conical thatched roofs, their farms linked by tracks. The longer drove roads allowed stock to pass between seasonal grazing areas from the lowland mosses to the high hills. The Brigantes only massed together for ceremonial purposes or to form a powerful guerrilla army in the event of war. They were famously rebellious when the Romans first arrived in the area, and lived resentfully under military occupation.

The Romans paved many of the existing thoroughfares and the pattern of settlements can hardly have altered much to this day. The valley landscape is still one of agriculture – small fields rising up to wilder hill country, with occasional patches of ancient hanging woods along various stretches of the river.

Many of the straggling grey stone villages built above the floodplain overlooking the Lune are built on ancient sites – Whittington's church of St Michael, with its stalwart fifteenth-century tower, stands on a castle mount. Together with Arkholme (pronounced 'Arkum'), whose lane leads down to a ferry which used

to cross to Melling on the opposite hillside above the wide water meadows beside the river, these villages form part of a cluster of defensive sites along the valley: the densest distribution of Norman castles outside the Welsh borders. The site of Castle Stede, now ruinous, commands the valley upstream to Melling, and half a mile downstream Hornby stands on a beautiful reach between the Lune and the Wenning, dominated by its castle on the tongue of land between the two valleys.

One of the great wonders of the canal world is the sixty-foot-long aqueduct designed by John Rennie and built at the end of the eighteenth century, which carries the Lancaster Canal over the River Lune. This great feat of engineering did not grab the attention of the artists of the day. Instead they turned their attentions to the view at the 'Crook o' the Lune', an extravagant loop of the river where a red-brick bridge crosses between Caton and Halton. This now-famous beauty spot, with its official 'picnic site', was immortalised by Turner and by the poets Gray and Wordsworth. Upstream, where the 'Devil's Bridge' spans the Lune at the market town of Kirby Lonsdale, Ruskin declared, 'I do not know in all my country, still less in France or Italy, a place more naturally divine.'

Charlotte Brontë, on the other hand, who attended the clergy daughters' school nearby at Cowan Bridge with her sister Anne, did not see the Lune Valley in such romantic terms. She immortalised the school in *Jane Eyre* as the harshly disciplined 'Lowood', and St John the Baptist's church at Tunstall overlooking the Lune became 'Brocklebridge'. 'My first quarter at Lowood seemed an age; and not the golden age either … Sundays were dreary days in that wintry season. We had to walk two miles to Brocklebridge church where our patron officiated. We set out cold, we arrived at church colder; during the morning service we became almost paralysed.'

Left: the Lune Valley near Whittington

119

Lydney, Gloucestershire

Lydney is in that far-flung corner of Gloucestershire north of the Severn Bridge, so removed from the golden, glamorised Cotswolds that it might as well be a foreign country. On the main street of this plain little town, The Archive Shop, opposite the garage, specialises in transport history and is packed on a weekend. Train buffs look in here on the way to see the Dean Forest Railway, which used to run from the heart of the forest to Lydney Docks. Before the coal mines were closed down, the coal was transferred from there to barges which navigated the short distance on the Lyd to meet the mighty Severn. Now a straggling industrial estate has crept across the willowy meadows along Lydney Harbour, and the sensationally beautiful Naas House stands decaying and abandoned.

Two miles from here in Lydney Park, up in the fringes of the mysterious Forest of Dean, is one of the most romantic places in England. Secreted high on the spur of Camp Hill and secure within the defences of an Iron Age hill fort are the remains of a Roman temple to the god Nodens. Above and around are huge ancient oaks, beeches and sweet chestnuts. A flight of steps leads up to the remains of a Roman guesthouse laid out round a central courtyard, and a herd of fallow deer graze among the ruins of a row of baths. From here you can see miles of the wide and shimmering River Severn, and across the Vale of Berkeley on its southern side to the distant line of the Cotswold hills on the horizon.

The temple has long been a secret place. It remained virtually untouched until it was excavated in the early 1800s by members of the Bathurst family, who owned the surrounding estate. They found caches of bracelets, rings, coins and ornaments, including the most exquisite bronze figure of a sleeping lurcher. All had been left as votive offerings to Nodens, god of the river and of healing. The archaeologist Sir Mortimer Wheeler dug the site over a century later on what is locally known as Dwarf's Hill, and at one point was assisted by his friend J R R Tolkien. The area, riddled with tunnels and the remains of open-cast mines, is said to have been the inspiration for the Shire in *The Hobbit*.

The archaeological finds are displayed in a small museum in the Bathursts' gabled Victorian pile, set across the deep-cut valley opposite. Also in the collection are some eccentric memorabilia from New Zealand, where Charles Bathurst, first Viscount Bledisloe and renowned agriculturalist and cattle-breeder, was Governor General in the 1920s. On his return from New Zealand he planted a group of 'Cynthia' rhododendrons high at the head of this dramatic and magical valley. The soil is not suitable for acid-loving plants like rhododendrons, but the depth of the old forest leaf mould is such that they flourish. In 1957 the second Viscount planted and nurtured eight acres of rare rhododendrons, azaleas and Japanese acers down the valley, with its water-falling stream and terraced pool. Today it is the nearest thing in Britain to walking in the foothills of the Himalayas. You can climb up and up on winding paths and look down the steep valley sides on clouds of colour. Some of the *Rhododendron macabeanum* leaves are as big as dinner plates, and the smell of the 'Loderi King George' is wonderfully heady. Appropriately, the Bledisloes have traditionally been Verderers of the Forest of Dean, protecting the rights of the people of the Forest, which include the grazing of animals and the digging of surface mines. They meet twice yearly in Speech House, Cinderford.

Right: the remains of a Roman temple in Lydney Park

The Manifold Valley, **Staffordshire**

Staffordshire is an intriguing county. Few talk of its cathedral, its parish churches, its great houses, or its castles. We may all know about Stoke-on-Trent, but to some outsiders the rest of Staffordshire remains a mystery.

There are great tracts of the White Peak District which belong not, as many assume, to Derbyshire, but to Staffordshire. It is here that you can find some of the most dazzling landscape in the British Isles. High limestone plateaux are crisscrossed with silvery stone walls and deeply incised with wooded river valleys where waterfalls crash over boulders and alders hang to precipitous banks. It is wild country – an English Switzerland.

I looked for Wetton in the drizzle, twisting and turning between strangely shaped hills, outcrops of rock and dells scattered with crimson-berried hawthorns. Clumps of leafless trees, black against the watery sky, looked like seaweed. The village of Wetton lies isolated on top of the moors. Lonely roads lead to it from Butterton, Alstonefield and Grindon. It is set on a gentle slope, its sturdy houses and cottages built of the local elephant-grey limestone, its pub, Ye Olde Royal Oak, whitewashed and welcoming. A red tractor chugged past down the hill as I walked through the lychgate, past graves of Cantrells, Wints and Bestwicks, to the solid Gothic box of a church. It was built in 1820 to replace one lost in a fire. The Victorian school alongside has been converted into the village hall, the Methodist chapel (Primitive Methodism was founded in Staffordshire) remains untouched. At either end of the village there are fine barns, some converted into holiday cottages.

Wetton is a perfect place from which to explore the wonders of the Manifold Valley. Its river rises at Flash Head just south of the River Dove and meanders through uneventful gritstone country before it sweeps past Ecton Hill, once the site of the most productive copper mines in England. From here on the limestone country begins and the river winds on through a spectacular gorge directly below Wetton. A trickle of a lane leads from the village between moss-covered stone walls into this magical valley. As the lane grows steeper it becomes almost pitch-dark under trees hung thick with ivy. The hills all around are snaked with walls and dotted with small stone barns and patches of gorse. Butterton church spire pierces the skyline ahead.

A rocky crag, like a mini Matterhorn, strikes three hundred feet up from the river bed and can be seen from miles around. Near the summit, the eerie Thor's Cave – a huge gaping hole in the rock face – has been inhabited by animals and man for over four thousand years. In the mid-nineteenth century, Samuel Carrington of Wetton and his friend Thomas Bateman of Hartington excavated this and other nearby caves and barrows. In Thor's Cave they found the bones of cave lions, bison, rhinoceros and three species of bear, as well as bronze and amber artefacts, beaker pottery, Saxon coins and jewellery.

One of the most unusual narrow-gauge lines, the Leek and Manifold Valley Light Railway, once made its way down this section of the Valley. It took forty-five minutes to travel the eight odd miles. The line was never a financial success and the last train ran on Saturday March 10th 1934 when there were several inches of snow lying. To those who loved the railway it was a melancholy day. The track bed is now part-footpath and part-narrow road, leading down the ever-deeper and grander valley unfurling towards the ghost of a station at Wetton Mill.

Right: Thor's Cave in the Manifold Valley

Mapperton, Dorset

Mapperton is out of the way. A few miles back from the red sandstone-cliffed sea, it lies hidden among small rounded hills – like an English Tuscany, but richly green and studded with small woods. It is just as the great pastoral poet William Barnes described in his Dorset dialect, 'No plough, soft deepenst Dorset'.

Whether you approach Mapperton from the pretty market town of Beaminster or winding up Mythe Hill from Melplash on unadopted lanes, its position at the head of a sudden and secret valley is a complete surprise. You approach the house down a short straight drive, which leads you to its west front. The entrance court is like a small hamlet huddling round the house – barns, a dovecote, a chapel and two eagle-topped gate piers. A little apart are two ravishing Renaissance stable blocks which continue the courtyard effect and lead your eye out over a ha-ha to fields. The whole harmonious composition of buildings is built in varying shades of golden stone.

Until this century, Mapperton had a long history of unbroken occupation in continuous descent from the family of Brett, or Bryte, who owned the manor in the time of Edward I, the Brodrepps, Comptons and Morgans, each inheriting through the female line. Robert Morgan of Mapperton was granted a licence by Henry IV to sit in his presence with a hat on because of 'diverse infirmities which he hath in his hedde and cannot conveniently, without his great daungier, be discovered of the same'. His grandson Robert built the present house in the middle of the sixteenth century, but over time it has been much changed from the original. Richard Brodrepp built the exquisite stable ranges and joined the original Tudor house to the church in the seventeenth century, and a fourth and last Richard Brodrepp classicised the north front in the eighteenth century.

It is only when you walk through to the eastern side of the house that you first glimpse Mapperton's hidden glory – from the plateau on which the house stands, a dramatic valley falls steeply away, winding in a long slow curving descent towards thick woods and the unknown pastures of blue, distant Dorset. From the house, and down the first slopes of the valley, there stretches a garden created in three completely different stages – but it rolls easily into a wonderful whole. Like the house, the garden has evolved over time – the same local stone has been used for walls and paving throughout, and topiary yew trees blend the varying dates of building.

At the head of the valley there is an elaborate Italianate garden which was made in the 1920s by the then owner, Mrs Labouchère, following the fashion of the day. Wide shallow steps lead down between gently banked lawns to terraces of early crazy paving. There are stepped octagonal rose-beds, statues, a pond choked with lilies, Roman columns, yew rooms, secret places and an inordinate number of composite stone storks. One huge step below is the seventeenth-century terrace where an Elizabethan garden house looks down onto two oblong carp ponds. The topiary yews have been added over the years. Below this is the latest garden of shrubs and trees started by Victor Montagu, former MP for South Dorset, in the 1950s, which is still being added to by his son and daughter-in-law with modern sculptures and new plantings. A path wanders on and on down the valley through young woodland and then zigzags on the far side back to the house.

Beyond the garden's edge, an old and long-abandoned drive leads for over a mile down the valley and away from Mapperton, through lost parkland and past a ruined mill beside a stream, past yellow flags and bright pink vetch until it eventually reaches the road to North Poorton.

Right: the west front of Mapperton House

Much Hadham, **Hertfordshire**

Hertfordshire is often ignored by aesthetes. They imagine it all roads, housing estates, industrial zones and new towns. This is not true. There is quiet rurality around Much Hadham, 'aristocrat of the county's villages'. Peaceful lanes dip and twist through this mild corner of England, which spreads its gently rolling hills in a great wide stretch, bounded by Ware, Harlow, Bishop's Stortford and Standon. Here is true, unadulterated Hertfordshire. You can walk for twenty miles across country without encountering a single village. Huge, dark and secret woods, like Plashes and Sawtress Wood, border the River Rib, which meanders north, crisscrossed by fords. There are ancient and remote farmhouses, gabled and whitewashed, with black-boarded barns huddled round the yard, and all about pasture, plough, little copses and muddy tracks.

The River Ash winds through this comfortable country along a little valley, and the road following its course leads you from Ware through the pretty village of Wareside and on to Widford, with its lonely church set a little apart from its community. You can see the neat recessed spire, like a child's drawing of a church, from miles away. Near the churchyard, a track leads past Thistly Wood to Fillets Farm and the road runs on past small cottages, some half-timbered, some pargeted, many white-washed, and The Green Man pub, colour-washed in green. All is modest and on a modest scale.

Henry Moore loved this stretch of Hertfordshire. In 1940 he found a house to rent in the hamlet of Perry Green, and stayed there until his death forty-five years later. His spirit still pervades not only Perry Green, where the Henry Moore Foundation has its headquarters, but also the elegant cloistered church of St Andrew's in Much Hadham, where his blankly haunting King and Queen, carved in 1953, stare from either side of the west door. His stained glass, wrought by the celebrated stained-glass maker Patrick Reyntiens and his son, is strange and magical and fills the west-end

window with shades of blue and the black branches of a tree in winter, against a watery sky beneath. The church kneelers too are a work of art, made by the villagers themselves. Much Hadham's houses and cottages are depicted in every detail in needlework, as are horses, kingfishers, tractors, butterflies and flowers. I visited on a Sunday morning and there was a traffic jam of church-goers in the back lane beside the shaded river – the church of St Andrew's is used by both the Church of England and Roman Catholics. A topiary cat in privet leant against a cottage and there was the steepest cat's-slide thatched roof I have ever seen.

The red-brick village hall with its Sixties extension was housing a craft fair, where quietly-spoken women sold cakes and home knits, and outside, Much Hadham's mile-long, sinuous street stretched away in late Sunday morning emptiness: colour-washed houses and cottages of lemon or blue or white, some half-timbered, some with over-sailing upper floors; grand gabled houses; a glamorous red-brick Georgian hall and stables; a Bishop's Palace, which the Bishops of London used as their country residence for eight hundred years and where Edmund Tudor, father of Henry VII, was born in 1431; a cricket pitch; the elegant Regency Gothic ('White') house; old drapers', bakers' and collar-makers' houses and shops; cobbled pavements; sentinel box and bay trees outside front doors of the well-to-do; a fire engine; almshouses; a Spar shop; two pubs where you can hear talk of the Pet Shop Boys who lived in Much Hadham; an old forge; much red-berried cotoneaster; polished brass knockers; red-pantiled roofs telling of East Anglia and classy pargeting (decorative plasterwork) on many of the older houses in the local style of geometric squares.

Right: the mile-long main street in Much Hadham

126

North Bovey, **Devon**

The inimitable character of large tracts of rural Devon has survived miraculously intact. It is deep-set, safeguarded by its centuries-old farming traditions. The terrain dictates the way men fashion it and Devon's ten thousand miles of lanes cannot easily be tidied up with kerbstones and widened to suit Euro lorries, for – particularly in North Devon – their paths are too deep and sinuous, and the hills over which they snake too steep. The nature of the lanes makes any hurry impossible.

North Bovey (pronounced to rhyme with 'luvvie') is famously hard to find. The sunken lanes all around are like switchbacks dipping into shady hollows and climbing precipitously between high earth or stone-faced banks topped with hedges. Sometimes wind-blown trees or overgrown hedges tunnel you into darkness. Many of these 'Devon Hedges' are a thousand years old or more, and thanks to their protective winter shelter harbour the most luxuriant flora imaginable: snowdrops, violets, primroses, bluebells, campion, early purple orchids, dog roses, honeysuckle, bell flowers, ferns, meadowsweet and sometimes sudden patches of purple columbine, to name a few of hundreds. Glimpses of rich landscape – distant mossy woods, patchworks of small fields or sudden outcrops of moorland granite – appear fleetingly through gateways, and very soon you have lost all sense of direction. The crossroads seldom have signposts but it is only the foreigners who need them. The old tin mines of Birch Tor and East Birch Tor, North Bovey's main industry for five hundred years, closed a century ago and lie abandoned, while hidden, un-dateable cob longhouses nestle into the hillside in bosky dells.

As the huge heights of Easdon Tor began to fill the southern sky, suddenly, as though by magic, I found myself right in the middle of North Bovey's sheltered fold. The village grows from the landscape. Its thatched cottages of whitewashed cob and granite are clustered together round the small green, where a pump, an ancient cross, a mounting-block and a scattering of lichen-covered oaks complete a perfect picture of Devon. To a Devonian the word 'cob' resonates with images of home. Nowhere in England is there so much mud building as there is here. The combination of perfect raw ingredients in the local soil and the perfection of local building traditions over centuries made cob the prime building material from the fourteenth to the nineteenth centuries. The village hall on the top side of the green is thatched, the Methodist chapel converted into a home, and The Ring of Bells Inn (the former manor) is hidden behind cottages and reached across a courtyard. It is an 'un-themed' free house with a genuine Devon air.

The fifteenth-century moorland church of St John stands consolingly on a knoll above the green. It has silvery granite columns, whitewashed walls, beautiful carved bench-ends, a barrel-vaulted ceiling, and ancient bosses, one with three rabbits carved into it, their ears meeting and forming a triangle, symbolic of the trinity.

In the late nineteenth century, a member of the W H Smith family bought the whole village and surrounding estate, and in 1907 proceeded to build a new manor-house a quarter of a mile away in the form of a gigantic mock-Jacobean mansion (now a spa hotel), the park and a golf course. He built cottages for his staff in the village, but the character of North Bovey was hardly changed.

The steepest lane out of North Bovey, past curving garden walls stuffed with ivy-leaved toadflax and valerian, leads to a ford where the dark gold river carves its way under alders down to Bovey Tracey. Further upstream a narrow stone bridge undulates across a marshy meadow and leads to Manaton where, in the church, there is a wonderful stained-glass window by the artist Frank Brangwyn of surpliced choirboys among lush greenery and foxgloves, the Devon hedge perhaps its inspiration.

Right: St John's Church stands on a knoll beyond the village green

The Oxford Canal

The Oxford Canal is a source of wonder. Whether it is cutting through the heart of an industrial town, past long back gardens strung with lines of washing, factories and allotments, or past the wide fields, woods, battlefields and sylvan villages of Warwickshire, Northamptonshire and Oxfordshire, it is an awe-inspiring feat of engineering. Its legendary designer James Brindley was born in 1716 in a small farm cottage near Buxton in Derbyshire, the eldest of seven children, and at seventeen became an apprentice to a millwright, where he gained a reputation for mending broken machinery. His fascination with water and engineering led him to be employed in the creation of the Bridgewater Canal. He set up his own business in Leek in Staffordshire and went on to build nearly three hundred miles of England's canal system, including the Grand Trunk and the Chesterfield, Birmingham and Oxford Canals. At forty-nine he married nineteen-year-old Anne Henshall. Six years later, while surveying a new branch of the Trent and Mersey Canal, he got soaked to the skin in a rainstorm, caught a chill and retired to a damp bed in a local pub. He was dead within days and never saw the completion of the Oxford Canal, which was opened 1790.

The eighty-mile-long waterway was once a main artery of trade between London and the Midlands, linking the Thames at Oxford with the Grand Union and Coventry Canals at Coventry. It was built over a period of twenty years, but by the time it got to Napton the Oxford Canal Company was desperately short of money. The final stretch north of Oxford had to be skimped on. Swing bridges were used instead of expensive brick ones and stretches of the Cherwell were incorporated into the canal. When the Grand Union Canal was finished in 1810 it became the favoured route between the Midlands and Oxford. The Oxford Canal's heyday was over. Lately it has had a renaissance as a recreational waterway.

I travelled a short stretch north of Oxford, past the hamlet of Thrupp where a long row of canal cottages, built of the local grey-gold limestone, lines the narrow lane alongside. A dozen barges are moored to the bank and The Boat Inn still serves bargees as it has always done. At weekends it is packed with waterways enthusiasts. A swing bridge, levered open by leaning on its long arms, leads to an eighteenth-century canal maintenance yard. The stables, workshops and thatched cottages are now owned by British Waterways. Next to the yard the canal opens into a large pool. The railway runs parallel to the canal across willowy meadows on an embankment, and soon the River Cherwell rushes downstream, flooding the fields around and marooning the alders. It's a slow, silent world until the next train streaks by, bound for Leamington Spa or Oxford. The canal slowly curves around Shipton-on-Cherwell, where back gardens slope towards the water's edge ending in small jetties and idiosyncratic summer houses. In a field nearby, the remains of a cetiosaurus, a twenty-yard-long dinosaur, were recently discovered.

Further on, stranded beside the river, the railway and the canal, are the remains of the lost village of Hampton Gay. Only the church and the manor farmhouse remain beside the gaunt ruins of an Elizabethan mansion. The village, once prosperous through its steam-powered paper mill, was all but deserted after it suffered a double disaster in the 1880s: the mill closed and the mansion was gutted by fire. They say that a curse was put on the owner of the property when he refused to give shelter to survivors of the terrible rail crash of 1874. A Great Western train came flying off the bridge at Hampton Gay and thirty-one people were killed. Willows and may trees line the long silent stretch to Somerton Deep Lock where, over two hundred years after it was built, Brindley's brilliance remains untarnished. It lies marooned in fields with its green-shuttered lock-keeper's cottage beside, a mile from any road.

Left: Upper Heyford Lock in Oxfordshire

Right: the cloisters in
the Peto Garden
Inset: Iford Manor with
the statue of Britannia in
the foreground

The Peto Garden, Iford Manor, Wiltshire

In the deep valley of the River Frome, where Somerset meets Wiltshire, there is a corner of Italy. A fifteenth-century bridge, built by the monks of Hinton Charterhouse, leads to an idyllic manor house, which Harold Ainsworth Peto found in 1899 like a 'sleeping beauty' and where he decided to create the garden of a lifetime. A bold statue of Britannia, erected by Peto, stands in the middle of the bridge and demonstrates this unusual gardener's genius for creating magic through incongruity.

Peto enjoyed a successful architectural partnership with Ernest George but became increasingly interested in garden design in his latter years. His stylish water gardens at Buscot Park in Oxfordshire were much admired and generated commissions all over England and in the south of France. Iford Manor's garden, his own, remains his masterpiece. He restored the rambling ancient back regions of the house in accord with William Morris's ideal of medieval tranquillity, retaining the grander eighteenth-century formality at the front. The Romans, who had a knack for choosing perfect building sites, had been here long before. For Peto, it was 'a haunt of ancient peace' and he immediately embarked on a manuscript which he called, in true Medieval Revival style, *The Boke of Iford*.

He believed that for the highest development of beauty a garden must contain both architecture and plants. 'Old buildings of masonry,' he wrote, 'carry one's mind back to the past in a way that a garden of flowers only cannot do. Gardens that are too stony are equally unsatisfactory; it is a combination of the two in just proportion which is the most satisfactory.'

The garden is as far from the beau ideal of an English country garden as you can get. No quaint haphazard rectory flowerbeds for Peto: 'It is difficult to understand,' he said, 'what pleasure anyone can derive from the ordinary herbaceous border ... without the slightest attempt at form, and the taller plants tied in a shapeless truss to a stake, and the most discordant colours huddled together.' He thought that the picture should be painted with hedges, canals, broad walks, with seats and statues and tall cypresses, and that the flowers were 'entirely subordinate'.

For thirty years Peto built his dream on this steep tumbling hillside. For years before, he had been an assiduous and discerning collector of ancient objects, and here at last was the perfect setting. When he first came, there was a series of grass terraces rising above the house and ending in a long, hanging wood, where now the King Edward VII column towers among the trees and commands the valley view. From the hanging wood, a long flight of steps leads down onto the Great Terrace, which is like a triumphal way paved with stone and lined on one side with a series of Ionic columns. Two oil jars shipped from Nice stand on either side of the steps. According to Peto, they were 'the largest I have ever seen. They arrived so damaged by their long journey that I had to put copper bands and rivets to hold them together.' Along the length of the terrace are bay trees in tubs, lions on plinths, a Greek sarcophagus, and the eastern end is stopped by a garden house which was moved from another site.

The gardens are full to the brim with Peto's trophies, languishing in cool colonnades and arbours, beside fountains and ponds, on pedestals and in niches. He believed that the French masons of the thirteenth and fourteenth centuries had reached the summit of the Gothic spirit, and bought pieces which had come indirectly from the clerk of works in charge of the restoration of the Cathedral of Notre-Dame in Rheims. Perhaps his *pièce de résistance* is the cloisters, built in the Italian Romanesque style, using stone from a nearby disused bridle path. Thirteenth-century lions from Lombardy guard the entrance and inside there is a little courtyard containing fragments from Greece, Italy and France.

Rame, Cornwall

If you approach Rame along the wooded valley of the River Lynher and dip and twist through the village of Millbrook, you can take a narrow lane by way of the tiny hamlet of Wiggle. From hilltops and at the end of sudden valleys are glimpses of the sea. Ivy hangs from holly trees in the hedges and acres of bracken, brown in autumn, tumble down the cliffs. You pass a farm where a hanging sign sticks out into the road saying 'Rabbits – pet or plate' and travelling on up the cow-muck-spattered lane, past Rame Barton in its jumbled yard, there is a wonky rubble wall full of ivy-leaved toadflax and a gate leading to St Germanus's Church which serves the tiny hamlet and parish of Rame. Cornwall feels ancient – cut off from the rest of the world and Celtic through and through.

The church offers the last shelter before the desolate headland. It is dug deep into the hill to protect it from sea gales. Partly thirteenth-century, it is all built of rough slate and has a slender, unbuttressed tower and strange 'broached' spire. Inside, it reveals a double-aisled splendour, which is still lit only by candles. Its surrounding graveyard is huge, wild and unkempt. The headstones are packed tightly together, for this beautiful place high above the cliffs is a favourite burial place. A simple stone in the porch reads 'E O L Gone Home'.

There, on the very summit of the headland, is the small mariners' chapel of St Michael, which is built on the site of an earlier Celtic hermitage. It is a twenty-minute walk from the hamlet of Rame to the chapel. The narrow road passes a row of coastguards' cottages and ends on a blustery bluff beside a radio mast and lookout hut. A path across smooth turf and worn rocks continues steeply down and up again, a daunting route for the faint-hearted pilgrim on a winter's day. The chapel is three hundred feet up in the teeth of the wind. The east window, glassless, looks towards Plymouth Sound and to tiny specks of sails miles out to sea. Among countless pieces of graffiti wrought by local lovers, 'I LOVE MANDY' stands out from the rest, carved large and clear into the slate sill. Hawks hover at eye level above the surrounding precipitous slopes of bracken. Below, the ramparts of cliff drop sheer to the sea. Basking sharks lurk in these waters and in a big storm a single roller, built up from the Atlantic swell, falls with a pressure which weighs a ton on every square foot.

From the fifteenth century, until the Eddystone Lighthouse was built eight miles off the coast, Plymouth paid a watchman at Rame to maintain a beacon there to warn shipping and to bring news to the city of important ships.

In 1815 the HMS *Bellerophon*, with her infamous passenger Napoleon, was watched over from Rame while she was anchored in neighbouring Cawsand Bay for a month. After his escape from Elba and his recapture, the Emperor had been brought here under the misapprehension that an estate in England was being found for him to live in. His presence drew crowds from all over England. So many dinghies, rafts, barges and skiffs, filled with gawping onlookers, sailed out to where the *Bellerophon* lay that you could walk from Plymouth Hoe all the way to Cawsand on their decks. Wearing white gloves and a uniform he had had pressed in Plymouth especially for the occasion, Napoleon appeared on deck twice a day and waved to the assembled cheering masses.

When the crew finally shipped anchor and set sail, past Penlee Point from where the foghorn now moans, Rame Head was the last bit of England Napoleon set eyes on. He turned to Captain Maitland and said quietly, '*Enfin, ce beau pays.*'

Ramsholt, **Suffolk**

Australia's famous son, the painter Arthur Boyd, said that the low, tussocky expanses around his Ramsholt cottage reminded him of Down Under. There's a hard, watery light here, a wide sky. Ramsholt is an utterly isolated place, the last village in Suffolk where you can hear the purest form of the local dialect with its distinct lack of s's.

Four stalwart martello towers facing out to sea stand at strategic intervals from Shingle Street down to the mouth of the River Deben, and just inland across this lost, low-lying marshy country you find the small red-brick village of Alderton, surrounded by willows. A lane leads away to the west between sandy brown fields of young barley, destined for local maltings, and there ahead is the snaking, silver river, a mile wide, with a slow-curving sea wall protecting great stretches of bird country. Long before this marshland was drained, Edward III's fleet was moored at Goseford at the mouth of the estuary, once a large port. Only the ghost of it remains now, like the ghost of the lost city of Dunwich up the coast where church bells still ring out from under the sea on stormy nights. Suffolk is thick with ghosts, and M R James, who lived here for most of his life, further fuelled the flame with his terrifying stories like 'Whistle and I'll Come To You'. I wouldn't choose to go for a walk in the half-light down among the reeds and willows. But for a twitcher it is as near to paradise as he will ever get. During the great autumn migration every sort of wading bird and wildfowl stops off here.

Through heathy gorse country the lane from Alderton kinks near Peyton Hall and then tilts steeply down to Ramsholt Quay, where the metal rigging of the moored sailing boats clinks against their masts in the breeze and a lurcher/Airedale cross barks at the gate to the pink stucco pub beside. The pub is one of the last vestiges of what was once a thriving community. In the 1920s barges still brought coal to Ramsholt Dock, and George Cook, who lived at Hill House above the pub, took carrots across the river by boat once a week and then wheeled them in a wheelbarrow the six miles to Ipswich market.

From the sandy path above the river, where tamarisk and samphire grow, you can see a dozen rarer than rare avocets on the water, and where the river bends the sudden view of lonely All Saints church on the skyline is unforgettable. Beside it a deep-sunk bramble-edged track leads down to what was once Ramsholt village – now scrappy and lumpy rabbit land. There is valerian all over the churchyard, pale green lichen on the tombs, a round church tower, which could be Roman, box pews and a double-decker pulpit inside, and seventeen souls on the electoral roll, over half the community.

A little way on, beside Shottisham Creek, the drained pastures have recently been flooded again to encourage duck. In the 1880s a local self-made magnate called Sir Cuthbert Quilter bought this whole wedge of marshy country, built a flamboyant house at Bawdsey, and set about creating a perfect partridge shoot by planting small woods, copses and field edges of Scots pines. His family motto was '*Plutôt mourir que changer*'. He'd be glad to know that, apart from the Scots pines now towering into the Suffolk sky, his quiet corner of England has hardly changed a jot.

Right: Ramsholt Quay on the River Deben

Rendham, Suffolk

A few miles back from the salt marshes and the sea, Rendham straggles along the road between Framlingham and Saxmundham in a forgotten low-lying stretch of Suffolk. It is an unassuming place. Colour-washed and pantiled cottages line the main village street which doglegs around the silvery flint church and the huge graveyard with its towering clumps of Scots pine. Along the lane towards Bruisyard, new 'executive' homes creep across the water meadows in a feeble effort to simulate the Suffolk style, but nothing diminishes the beauty of the winding River Alde. It wanders beside the village on its way to the posher environs of wind-blown Aldeburgh, brimful of arty people running craft galleries, dedicated golfers and struggling novelists, all of them watching and worrying over their ever-shrinking shingle beach.

Rendham, on the other hand, lies safe and snug, unvisited by tourists in its mild valley, where the river's upper reaches are sheltered by coppiced alders as tall as oaks. A twenty-strong flock of Roman geese glides downstream or marches about the meadows. A few locals have seen otters on the riverbank. The river must have been a solace to the poet and naturalist George Crabbe who chose to live here in the early 1800s – 'Nature's sternest painter, yet the best,' said his ardent fan, Byron.

Born in Aldeburgh, the son of a tax collector, Crabbe's early and unsuccessful literary career was transformed by Edmund Burke, who got his poetry published to critical acclaim and advised him to join the clergy, thus guaranteeing a living and a rectory. Having been patronised by nobility in the West Country and the Midlands for more than twenty years, he decided to become curate of Swefling in his native Suffolk when he was in his mid-forties. Perhaps this was because his domestic circumstances were so dire and he felt safer here. He had lost five of his seven children, and when the latest child died his wife Sarah, the love of his life, became chronically depressed. Crabbe withdrew into himself,

reading books, particularly on botany, and studying beetles (he was an eminent coleopterist and found the first recorded specimen of *Calosoma sycophanta L* in Suffolk). Although his increasingly reclusive behaviour and neglect of his duties began to jeopardise his future as curate of Swefling, he managed to get a leave of absence from his boss, the Bishop of Lincoln. In 1801 he moved into a house in Rendham where he stayed for four years, taking opium on a regular basis for his digestion and beginning his famous poem 'The Borough', a series of lengthy letters in heroic couplets, one of which inspired Benjamin Britten's opera *Peter Grimes*.

Rendham has a long tradition of non-conformism. Apart from being fiercely Royalist during the Civil War, when its next-door neighbour Swefling, and indeed most of Suffolk, had sided with Cromwell, it also supported the Queen of the Iceni tribe, Boudicca, when she rallied troops from East Anglia to stand against the oppressive Roman occupation. Having taken the town of Colchester, legend has it that the victorious troops severed the bronze head of the Emperor Claudius from its body and used it as a football before they headed home. Whatever the truth, the head somehow landed in the Alde and was discovered in 1907 by a Rendham schoolboy called Arthur Godbold. The original is in the British Museum but there is a replica in Rendham church. Rendham's rebellious nature is further illustrated by its handsome Congregational chapel, the size of which denotes just how many dissenters from the orthodox church it attracted – sometimes up to six hundred. The four-square red-brick chapel, built in 1750 – it replaced an earlier one of a hundred years before – is now a private house.

Right: St Michael's Church, Rendham

Richmond, **Yorkshire**

I first saw Richmond from across the valley of the Swale. Cattle stood in the shade of enormous chestnut and beech trees, and the folds of hills are still wooded below the distant moors as they were in J M W Turner's day. I had walked from St Nicholas, an ancient rambling house where the famous gardener Bobbie James created a garden in the 1930s (a rose was named after him). The field before the house slopes down towards Easby – a ruined parish church, gatehouse and abbey beside the River Swale, which ripples down its stony bed, wide, brown and cool.

There can be few more beautiful views than the town on its rise, together with the ruined abbey a wooded mile downstream. On some days in winter, when the water pours off the moors, the river becomes a raging torrent and laps against the walls of the monastic buildings. There is an air of vanished splendour about the place – elaborate thirteenth-century interlacing arches, clustered columns, stiff-leaf capitals and quatrefoils carved above the doorway on the south front.

The town is clustered around the noble Norman castle. It was one of the country's first to be built in stone in 1071 and dominates all on its base of solid rock rising high above the river. Legend has it that King Arthur and his knights lie in a lost cave beneath it, the entrance of which is forever being searched for by romantics from Glastonbury. I prefer to think of King Arthur here rather than at Alderley Edge in Cheshire, the other claimant of the legend.

I walked round Richmond in the early evening, the cobbled streets were almost empty – some like New Street and Finkle Street were as steep to navigate as black ski-runs, each one ending with a magical view of distant moors or sheep- and tree-scattered hills. A winding lane led down the flank of rock past the handsome church, and the model public gardens were stuffed with standard roses rising from massed bedding in every gaudy shade. A spirit-lifter on grey days.

Behind the castle, at the very top of the hill, the market square spreads wide around the old market cross. Fine eighteenth-century houses abound and evidence of Richmond's past prosperity is everywhere. The market town first blossomed through being at the centre of the Swaledale sheep trade, and then through lead mining in nearby Arkengarthdale. The well-to-do came in droves to attend Richmond Races and to dance the evenings away at the Assembly Rooms, which are now the town hall. Richmond Grammar School's reputation shone bright when its two Georgian headmasters, Anthony Temple and, later, James Tate sent an inordinate number of their pupils to Oxford and Cambridge. Thirteen of Tate's classical scholars became fellows at Cambridge and were known as 'Tate's Invincibles'. Lewis Carroll attended the school in the 1840s when his father was vicar nearby.

Across the Queen Anne facade of the King's Head Hotel, I counted twelve window boxes and ten hanging baskets of trailing white petunias set against the pale pink brick. The town theatre, built in 1788, remains the most perfect Georgian theatre in Britain. This was because it closed down in 1848 and so escaped any Victorian makeover. In 1963 it was restored, and has lately been given a new lease of life.

Left: Richmond and its Norman castle

Rousham, Oxfordshire

The Gardens of Rousham are serene. A tree-shaded, single-tracked road leads through this obscure corner of golden-stoned Oxfordshire towards the magical domain. Turning in past a Victorian gate lodge of lichen-covered stone, the drive curves through the level park, where strawberry-roan longhorn cattle graze under huge trees and the stern facade of the house looks haughtily down its short avenue of weeping limes. Millefleur booted bantams, with feathers the colour of tortoiseshell butterflies, strut about the beautiful stable yard.

Rousham is the masterpiece of the designer William Kent (c.1684–1748). A true artist, he was miles ahead of his time and a forerunner of the Romantic Movement. His garden designs were a snub to the rigid formality of what had gone before. He did away with flowerbeds within sight of the house in order to give the impression that the surrounding lawns merged seamlessly into the park beyond. Animals were kept at bay by an invisible ha-ha, and everywhere was verdant glory.

William Kent was born in Bridlington in Yorkshire and began his apprenticeship as a coach painter. After a member of the local gentry had noticed his talent for painting, a group of Yorkshire squires raised some money to send him to Italy, accompanying the collector John Tellman. He was obviously an engaging character and soon made a lot of influential friends – among them the future Earl of Leicester, for whom he later built Holkham Hall in Norfolk, and the Earl of Burlington, with whom he became close friends and for whom he decorated Chiswick House and Burlington House. Burlington introduced Kent to the owner of Rousham, General James Dormer, an old soldier who had served with the Duke of Marlborough and had been Britain's minister in Lisbon. Dormer enjoyed the company of the fashionable artistic set of the day and often had figures like Swift, Pope and Horace Walpole to stay with him at Rousham. He recognised Kent's brilliance, and asked him to make alterations to his house and redesign his garden. 'If Kent can be persuaded to come I shall take it very kindly,' he said.

Pope's 'Genius of the Place' was duly consulted, and Kent created the magic that Rousham still possesses to this day. He dressed up the Jacobean house, built by Sir Robert Dormer, with a straight battlemented parapet, and glazed the windows with octagonal panes. He made low wings on the garden side with little Gothic ogee niches, and inside he embellished a small room with every trick in his book, from over-doors and over-mantels to swirly scrolls and swags.

Now matured to perfection, the garden remains exactly as he planned it. A mile away, on the near horizon, stands a sham ruin to act as an eye-catcher, and below it a mill, rendered romantically picturesque by Kent. Across the park to the west is a Palladian gateway beside a Cow Castle, with a stable on one side and a garden seat on the other. Kent dictated the way he wanted his visitors to walk, so that everywhere there were surprises and vistas. As Walpole wrote in a letter, 'The garden is Daphne in little, the sweetest little groves, streams, glades, porticoes, cascades and rivers imaginable; all the senses are perfectly classic.' Paths snake down the hill through haunting groves, giving sudden and unexpected views of sculptures, temples, pools and a long sinuous ribbon of water in a stone rill. The winding, alder-edged Cherwell bounds the garden, sometimes flooding the meadows beyond to form an enormous lake.

Nearer the house is a large walled garden with a tip-top herbaceous border, potting shed, dovecote, vegetable garden and central pond stuffed full of great-crested newts. Beside it is an old and romantic orchard, and rising just beyond is the church tower with its beautiful-sounding bells. General Dormer's descendants still live here and keep the garden in a state of quiet and peaceful perfection.

Left: the River Cherwell, which bounds the garden
Inset: part of Kent's seven-arched Praeneste

Royal Leamington Spa, Warwickshire

I went to Leamington Spa by train from Oxford through willowy meadows flooded with wide sheets of swan-studded water. The train follows the course of the River Cherwell and the Oxford Canal for nearly the whole journey, and at one point is joined by the M40 in an amazing intertwining of ways and methods of travel. You can see the ruined ancient manor and Georgian church of Hampton Gay close by the line, Rousham's crenellations above the trees, and the thrilling spire of King's Sutton church soaring above the village. Then the train strikes out on a series of embankments into the heart of Warwickshire. The station at Leamington was rebuilt in 1939 and has the most swanky chromium-plated double doors, just like the ones at Claridge's. They have been reinstated by the Railway Heritage Trust, as has the Art Deco lettering across the front of the station.

Spring is the best time to visit Leamington, when the trees are all freshly green and you can walk in the sun on a footpath around the back of the station, across Avenue Road with its grandly spaced veranda'd Regency villas and down to the River Leam and the Royal Pump Rooms, Leamington's *raison d'être*. At the end of the eighteenth century, Leamington was no more than a village, with its single spring still an undeveloped asset. In the wake of the success of Bath, a group of entrepreneurs got together and began to develop the town as a spa and promote the waters as having medicinal benefits. The first natural spring was supplemented by various wells which offered saline, sulphurous and chalybeate waters. Doctor Henry Jephson, an enlightened doctor, prescribed the waters of Leamington combined with a rigorous diet of plain food and a daily exercise regime as a natural cure-all. He drew not only Sarah Bernhardt, the Duke of Wellington and the poet Longfellow to the town, but also received Queen Victoria in 1838. Inevitably, visitors left Leamington feeling better: having been used to a rich diet, they had simply undergone a healthy detoxification.

The Jephson Gardens were created in the doctor's memory and form a lush green belt through the middle of the town, either side of the river. You can walk their length eastward, straight out into sheep-strewn fields beside the Leam and on along a footpath to the town of Warwick, which is virtually joined to Leamington.

Today, the results of that visionary Regency development of white and cream stucco terraces, squares and crescents, decked with elaborate wrought-iron balconies like fine lace, are still blooming. The atmosphere is uplifting and festive. There are trees everywhere, filling the squares and lining the wide, straight streets. Even the rows of different coloured cars – red, green, turquoise, white and silver – can look quite nice, parked under showers of almond-blossom trees along Newbold Terrace on the edge of Jephson Gardens. There are mature cedars and monkey puzzles, wonderful bedding displays, a bandstand on spacious lawns beside the river, and a wildly eccentric Victorian town hall. If you feel brave enough you can still take the waters from the original spring in the Pump Room, which has recently been converted into a brilliant art gallery and museum. It's just the right size and has some wonderful pictures: a smashing Robert Bevan, a John Piper, a Sickert, a Duncan Grant, a Henry Tuke of boys on a shingle beach, and a huge Lucy Kemp-Welch of cart-horses returning home from working the fields on a winter's evening. But the best of all is a sumptuous Ivon Hitchens called *Green Walk* – just right for Leamington.

Right: Jephson Gardens

144

St Germans, Cornwall

Once over the shimmering Tamar on Brunel's steel-spanned bridge at Plymouth, the train cuts through small hills and valleys high above Cornish fields. Past Trematon Castle, past Trehan and Trevollard, the line crosses the great tidal river of St Germans, high in the sky and over the most elegantly arched viaduct in the country. St Germans Quay below is spread with small fishing boats stranded on the low-tide mud and the village clusters up the hill to the south: a kingdom of its own on a peninsula. Along the northern bank the luxuriant pleasure gardens of Port Eliot slope down towards the river's edge and undulate away into faraway woods.

In the heart of the village, the train stops at a tiny station where two handsome railway buildings, painted blue and white, straddle the line. Comfortable Regency stucco houses beside them display gardens stuffed with blue hydrangeas, and once through the little picket gate the way leads into the village street. The houses and cottages all along it are built of the local mauvish-brown 'elvan' stone and soft woods rise steeply behind. The high garden walls of Port Eliot curl down one side of the street, protecting the place from the world and keeping it in a cocoon – it is even said to have its own micro-climate: if it's raining in Tideford, just up the road, it may not be raining here. Twenty years ago, a guidebook writer, annoyed at being unable to gain access to Port Eliot, wrote that 'a heavily feudal air hangs over the place'. He had glimpsed the gardens and the palm trees beside the orangery through cracks in the wall's locked door and heard tell of summerhouses and temples among magnolias and camellias. Too late for him, the gates to the house and garden are now open.

The Borough of St Germans itself grew up round the church dedicated to St Germanus, which served as the Cathedral of Cornwall from Saxon times. It remained the chief church in Cornwall until Truro Cathedral was built in the nineteenth century. Down a steep path off the village street, the church stands on a slope above Port Eliot. Its noble Norman west front, with two towers and central door under the grandest of dog-toothed arches, tells of its once powerful standing. Inside it is overwhelming. The sumptuous stained glass of the thirty-foot-high east window, greenery intertwining around biblical figures, is by Burne-Jones. Most dramatic of all is the monument in a side chapel to Edward Eliot, carved in 1722 by Rysbrack, which shows a man in Roman dress half-reclining while a woman looks down on him and cherubs fly above.

The Eliots, who were Cornish yeomen, bought Port Eliot in 1564. It was then a crumbling priory surrounded by rambling medieval buildings and overshadowed by the church. The tidal river reached the door and boats sailed past on the river inlet, giving the house its name of 'Port'. The view was not always idyllic: at low tide there were wide expanses of mud, and later Eliots employed Humphrey Repton to divert the river and transform the view into verdant parkland. Over the centuries the house grew organically around the early monastic vestiges and reached its architectural peak when the genius architect, Sir John Soane, was commissioned to beautify the place in the 1790s. He built reserved and elegant stables, farm buildings, a warehouse and lime kiln on the quay, and radically remodelled the interior of Port Eliot, giving it the graceful proportions it lacked. He added castellations to the exterior to harmonise with the church. Today the 'elvan' stone is silver with lichen and half the facades are smothered with magnolia grandiflora.

At the bottom of the village street there are some beautiful seventeenth-century almshouses, with wooden balconies, mullions, outer-steps and slate-hung gables.

Right: Brunel's viaduct and Cornwall's former Cathedral beside the house of Port Eliot

Salisbury Plain, **Wiltshire**

When you travel the lonelier tracts of Salisbury Plain the ghost of prehistoric man is always beside you. Scattered all over with his wood henges, cromlechs, earthworks and mounded graves, these wind-blown heights are engulfed in an almost audible silence. It is a primeval landscape from where, a hundred million years ago, wave upon wave of chalk downs began to form, now stretching away into Sussex, down through Dorset and north-eastwards to Berkshire. They rose above what had become the sea, the oldest hills of all, moulded in smooth, voluptuous folds by melting ice, and harbouring the first beginnings of our civilisation. Here in their midst, on a bleak, bare stretch, stands Stonehenge, the supreme monument of the Plain.

Perhaps because the water-table changed, the Saxons chose to move away and farm only the lower slopes of Salisbury Plain. For over a thousand years this high plateau became the haunt of shepherds whose flocks of sheep cropped the turf and kept the undergrowth at bay. Today, Salisbury Plain remains the largest area of untilled chalk downland in north-west Europe. The army has been its saviour from the plough. In 1897 they began buying up parcels of land to use as training grounds, and by the 1940s owned much of the Plain – a tenth of Wiltshire – stretching from Upavon in the north to Amesbury in the south, and from Ludgershall in the east to Westbury in the west. The outer circle of land around the Plain, where sheep still graze the steeper slopes and there are yellow brimstone and chalk-blue butterflies, is let by the MOD for farming. Further in, after a band of 'Schedule Three training land', the High Impact area begins – some of the wildest and remotest country in southern England. Hidden beyond shallow combes is the abandoned village of Imber on the Down, 'five miles from any town', which was requisitioned by the army in the 1940s. The villagers never returned, but once a year they are allowed to visit the church. It is used as a battle school. Sometimes you can hear the rumbling of an explosion and see smoke rising in the distance, and in the ensuing silence on a hot day in late summer, when the tufty grass is dry and yellowing and the oceans of treeless may– and-juniper–sprinkled downs stretch out forever, you could imagine yourself in the Serengeti Desert, with the distant smoke rising from some primitive settlement. The emptiness is overwhelming.

This isolated plateau, stretching over Great Fore and Chirton Down, Urchfont and Charlton Down, Can and Rushall Down, East Down and Honeydown, is cut through by the old coaching road from Devizes and Lavington to Salisbury, where the ghost of the highwayman Thomas Boulter, hanged in 1778, is often seen. When the red flags are not flying and the army is not practising warfare you can travel for miles into another world. It is so far from any chemical farming drift that a phenomenally rich and rare flora and fauna survive. There are Adonis Blue, Brown Hairstreak and Marsh Fritillary butterflies, burnt orchids, tawny bumblebees, soldier beetles, great-crested newts in the dew-ponds and nesting stone curlews camouflaged among tufts of grass. The bustards, which ran at fifty miles an hour, were hunted out a hundred years ago, but have now been reintroduced.

From east to west, the low-moaning A303 slashes through the middle of the Plain, a fleeting blur as though it were a thing apart. But the shallow river valleys of the Plain carry their winding roads, strung all along with villages and reedy willowy fields, to the hub of red-roofed Salisbury, capital of the Plain. For centuries the huge circular earthwork of Old Sarum on its strange mound on the town's northern skirt was the magnetic pull, but now the cathedral, with its soaring spire, commands the great watershed of the Plain.

Left: Urchfont Hill on the northern edge of Salisbury Plain

Salthouse, Norfolk

The wide-skied salt marshes on the edges of the cold North Sea are like some gigantic unfinished jigsaw of creeks and inlets among the eel grass, their far-stretching edges of greeny grey melting into the sea. The low-lying loneliness of this stretch of North Norfolk coast has long been a paradise for twitchers. For hour upon hour they will wait motionless, staring through their binoculars towards the sea or across the reedy, bird-haunted landscape for a glimpse of avocets, sedge warblers or reed warblers which come here to breed, along with skylarks, meadow pipits and lapwings.

This coast also inspires a band of faithful pilgrims who visit for their summer holidays and uphold the unchanging pattern of their days, whatever the weather. Followed by straggling children, they stake their territorial claim in the spot they always come to where the samphire grows beside the dunes. They walk for miles to reach the low tide-sea and shiver back across the rippled sand to huddle in their tribal camp and eat crab sandwiches sprinkled with tiny particles of grit.

Then when the breeze whips up in early evening the twitchers and beachcombers begin the complicated route home across the marshes, circumventing brackish lagoons and crisscrossing creeks and dykes to reach the wind-blown garden and the familiar holiday cottage with its swooping Dutch gables and pantiled roof.

At Salthouse, the ancient Peddars Way rides the high bank above the shingle beach, the only protection between land and sea. Over the centuries the village has shown a brave front to great storms, perhaps never more so than in 1897 when a contemporary account describes how between eight o'clock and noon the crests of the breakers were visible to an unusual extent above the ridge of the sea wall. 'Presently rent was made, speedily to be followed by others, and mighty waves coursed inland, filling the dykes and flooding the marshes. To such a height did the water rise that waves in some cases broke against the upper storeys of the houses. Furniture was washed away, fowls were drowned by the hundred and villagers had to be taken out of their bedroom windows by boats.' Salthouse suffered similar devastation in the great storm of 1953.

The church of Saint Nicholas stood firm. Sir Henry Heydon, a fifteenth-century property magnate who loved Salthouse, built it as high as he could on the sandy hillside in order to escape the floods, and also to act as a lighthouse to ships on this sometimes treacherous sea. He died in 1503, the year it was completed, but left one of the wonders of Norfolk to posterity – the soaring, triple-aisled, light-filled church with its clear glass clerestory and long and simple Perpendicular windows. 'What would you be, you wide East Anglian sky, without church towers to recognise you by? What centuries of faith, in flint and stone, wait in this watery landscape, all alone?' said my dad in his commentary for *A Passion for Churches*. No county has such a wealth of good churches, no coastline such a rich collection.

Past the church, the whitewashed Dun Cow pub, the grey pebble cottages, the footpaths and winding garden walls of Salthouse (once prosperous when salt was a valuable commodity), a lane leads up and up the sharply rising ridge of what were once cliffs along an earlier shore. Here on the heights of Salthouse Heath, this gorsey, heathery heathland high above the sea is scattered with burial mounds, including Three Halfpenny Hill and Three Farthing Hill. Beyond them is a cluster of over thirty barrows – the largest Bronze Age cemetery in Norfolk.

Left: Salthouse Church seen from Salthouse Heath

The Sapperton Canal Tunnel, Gloucestershire

Not far from the source of the Thames a strange circular lengthsman's cottage, like a squat pepper pot, appears above the brambles beside the vestiges of the Thames and Severn Canal. (A 'lengthsman' was responsible for the upkeep of a certain stretch of road, railway or canal.) Nearby, an unmetalled track, high above the deep, steep canal cutting called King's Reach, leads to the eastern entrance of one of England's greatest canal tunnels. Between the flat fields of north Wiltshire and the deep dark wooded valleys towards Bisley, it burrows through the Cotswold escarpment. Constructed by hand in the late eighteenth century, the Sapperton Canal Tunnel was, at the time, the biggest engineering achievement and the longest tunnel in the world.

The Thames and Severn Canal was never a commercial success. It was designed to link the two great rivers so that cheaper coal from the North and north-western collieries could reach the ever-mushrooming city of London. From the Thames at Inglesham the canal rose 343 feet through sixteen locks on its twenty-one-mile journey to the Severn. Soon after it was inaugurated, the Oxford Canal opened and took a lot of its trade, and when the railway finally came in 1840, the Thames and Severn began its slow and inevitable decline. It was abandoned in 1927 and left to nature.

This eastern portal to the tunnel, however, with its huge blocks of rusticated stone, its columns and pediment, became a haunt for pilgrims in search of the romantic. The niches, originally intended for statues of Father Thames and Madam Sabrina, became smothered in ivy; fallen beech trees lay spread-eagled across the cutting; and the tunnel's entrance, choked with black mud, looked like the gate to Hades. Before it was damaged by fire the Tunnel House Inn beside it used to be three storeys high, having been built in the 1780s to house some of the numerous tunnel workers.

Cutting the 3,817-yard (2.2-mile) tunnel through the escarpment was the most extraordinary and heroic feat. Though the numbers killed in the process were never recorded, the quantity of headstones erected in the local graveyards swelled considerably during the time of the tunnel's construction. The names carved on them are those of the miners who came from coal and tin mines in Derbyshire, Somerset and Cornwall. Their mining experience was invaluable to the engineers in charge, Josiah Clowes and Robert Whitworth. The initial contractor employed by the canal company, Charles 'Feckless' Jones, agreed a price of seven guineas a yard for a fifteen-foot-diameter bore and pledged to finish the tunnel in four years. Several contractors later, it was finished in five. In April 1789 the first shipments of coal were 'legged' through (men lay on top of the barge roof and 'walked' along the tunnel's ceiling) from the western end at the idyllic village of Sapperton, bastion of the Arts and Crafts movement at the turn of the century. Sapperton's portal, though castellated, is less spectacular.

Over the last few years the Cotswold Canals Trust has cleared the long cutting with its cathedral-like nave of beeches, and runs trips in a silent, flat-bottomed boat a third of the way down the tunnel. It was an eerie and magical experience for me, gliding in the ice-blue, crystal-clear water on and on into the darkness, through the hollowed-out golden limestone, until the light at the end of the tunnel becomes a pin-prick. In its middle section the canal becomes unnavigable. The bed of fuller's earth through which it passes caused subsidence problems from the outset. Anyway, by this time, as the odd drip of water from the palest pink stalactite hit my neck, I was quite pleased to be heading back into the light.

Right: the eastern portal of the tunnel

Shap, **Cumbria**

The village of Shap stretches either side of the old A6 at one of its wildest and highest points, 1,350 feet above sea-level. The west coast railway line from London to Glasgow slices in a slow curve beside it and in winter the faint roar of traffic on the M6 close by is often drowned by the wind. In the far distance tiny triangles of dark green fir woods are dotted across the looming brown fells, and beyond Loadpot Hill, unseen Ullswater curls its gloomy depths. Only an old Land Rover with several sheep dogs in the back is ahead of me on the motorway slip road, juddering past the lime works with its gigantic chimneys belching clouds of smoke, past the sign to Wet Sleddale – a tiny scattering of farms in a patch of emerald below – and on into the long, long grey-stone village of Shap.

Over the centuries it has grown up beside the old road to Scotland with a proliferation of inns and B&Bs – The King's Arms, The Bull's Head, the Greyhound Hotel, with a beautiful stone greyhound lying across the top of its porch, and the Hermitage with its whitewashed walls and black window surrounds in true Westmorland style. Since time immemorial travellers have been stranded here in the snow, and that feeling of camaraderie induced through complete strangers being thrown together on a stormy night still hovers. Though inordinately long and thin, the village has a cohesion about it and a strong community spirit – perhaps more so than ever since the M6 stole almost all of its trade. The little wooden pavilion with a shingle roof stands proud in Shap Memorial Park, and between the 1931 Methodist church and the fire station are chippies, Indian takeaways and coffee shops. In the oldest part of the street the buildings are smaller and seem to huddle together against the cold: The Crown Inn is tiny and snug, and the seventeenth-century market house, arched and beautiful, feels as though it was built for pygmies. It is now the library and its noticeboard displays what's on at the cinema in Keswick and a list of the services at St Margaret's Church, hidden behind the main street.

At the northern end of Shap a gated road leads to the jewel in the village's crown. Snow lies on the highest fells and black-faced sheep in the fields. Huge chunks of granite serve as gate posts, and pale green lichen the colour of pistachio ice-cream clings to the perfectly built stone walls which crisscross the landscape in thick silver threads. The lane leads for half a mile down into a soft and magical valley where the River Lowther wends a shallow, rocky, mossy way below hanging ash and alder. On the western bank in a small clearing is the ruined Abbey of Shap. It was founded in about 1191 by Premonstratensian canons. What remains of the church, begun in the thirteenth century, faces east towards the river, and the cloister, sacristy and chapter house to the south, reaching to the river bank. After the Dissolution the buildings were used as barns and as a local stone quarry. Only the Perpendicular tower, more difficult to demolish, was left to stand upright.

A farm is huddled close to the south side of the ruins, half made from the Abbey's stone – a cosy house with a saint's head carving over the door and ivy-clad walls, and a range of small barns, one with stone steps leading up to the granary. Altogether it is a beautiful place. The sense of continuity is strong, as is the sense of peace. There are two stone circles nearby and a little barn-like chapel connected to the abbey at Keld, a mile south.

Left: the ruined Shap Abbey

Shobdon Church, Herefordshire

Shobdon was the first church I ever really liked. I was twelve years old when I saw it. To me it looked like the most extravagantly glamorous drawing-room I had ever seen in my life. Filled with light, its swirling rococo plasterwork and its fancy décor of chalk-white walls, ice blue/grey paintwork and red-cushioned pews constituted the polar opposite of what I thought a church should look like. There was no hint of gloom and not much hint of God either. It seemed likely that a cocktail party might take place there at any minute. As the Shell Guide describes it, it would be an inconceivable place to hold a funeral.

Every time I have visited it over the years I still experience the same burst of surprise on entering, mixed with a feeling of slightly guilty pleasure. Sir John Bateman, who inherited the Shobdon estate in 1744 when he was twenty-three, preferred to lead an illustrious life in London than moulder away in Herefordshire. He left the estate management to his fashionable uncle Richard Bateman and delegated the design and overseeing of the building work of the new church almost entirely to him. Richard 'Dicky' Bateman was a friend of Horace Walpole, the writer, politician and architectural innovator, and together with a circle of like-minded cultivated and artistic thinkers, was a peripheral member of the 'Committee of Taste'. The latter's likely involvement with the design of the new church at Shobdon guaranteed a serious flight of fancy.

Horace Walpole had just enlarged his villa at Strawberry Hill in Richmond and had set a daring design precedent, aided and abetted by another committee member, the artist Richard Bentley, who was responsible for much of Strawberry Hill's decoration. Dicky Bateman, who owned a villa further up the Thames at Old Windsor, was keen to follow in the same artistic footsteps. The existing and, by all accounts, magnificent Norman church at Shobdon (said to be as fine as Kilpeck) was duly pulled down to make way for the dazzling new structure. Even at the time this was considered architectural sacrilege by traditionalists and antiquarians up and down the land. They were further aggrieved to see the great Romanesque chancel with its perfect dog-tooth design together with two doorways re-erected as a folly – a mere fashionable landscape ornament. Over the years some of the intricate carving by the famous Herefordshire School was lost to the weather, standing as it does on a rise to form a *point de vue* at the end of an avenue. Today the arches still look uncomfortable and out of place.

When you come out of the church there is a strange atmosphere. The gigantic Queen Anne mansion which stood nearby was demolished in 1933. Originally built in the style of Clarendon House by Sir James Bateman, sometime Mayor of London, who bought the estate in 1705, it stood on a long arcaded terrace looking out across the shallow valley of the River Lugg towards Presteigne and the Welsh hills beyond. The forlorn gate piers of the house and the eighteenth-century stables survive, and although Shobdon Hill Wood rises in a great protective sweep to the north, there is still an air of emptiness about the place.

Right: the interior of Shobdon Church

Sidmouth, **Devon**

Approach Sidmouth on a fine day by the small road from the west and travel through the thick beech woods of Peak Hill. Five hundred feet above the sea, the first sight of the town below and the slow arched shoreline between the towering red cliffs takes your breath away. It is the nearest thing to the Italian Riviera we possess. The climate is remarkably mild, as the town lies in a tree-clothed valley whose hills, behind the sea, rise higher than the cliffs. In winter Sidmouth is six degrees warmer than London and has less rainfall than any other south-coast resort.

Until its rarefied resort life began, Sidmouth was never an important place, although its port at the mouth of the River Sid is grandly called Port Royal. During the seventeenth century the river was 'choaked with chisel and sands by the viscitudes [sic] of the tides', but in 1795 Emmanuel Lousada, an enterprising Jewish businessman, saw Sidmouth and decided to convert it into the most elegant and genteel resort in England, a sort of Cheltenham-on-Sea. He bought up a lot of land and set a high standard of fanciful architectural design by building Sidmouth's first *cottage orné*, Peak Hill House (an ornately-designed small country house built in rustic style), high on a plateau near the cliff's edge. He then began advertising the glories of this sensational spot.

Watering places were by now becoming all the rage, and sea bathing was prescribed as being most healthy in mid-winter, preceded by the drinking of a quart of seawater. Although the first 'water cures' had been prescribed as early as 1660 by Dr Wittie, who had also promoted England's first resort of Scarborough, there were many doctors in the eighteenth century who suggested that seawater could cure everything from asthma to deafness. This led to a move towards the sea by the richer classes, ever vigilant of their health, and many resorts had doctors for promoters. Once the aristocracy and a member of the royal family had given their seal of approval, the resort took off. Sidmouth was a perfect success story. Mr Lousada was a brilliant publicist and gradually grand folk from the West Country and even further afield began to build holiday houses on the wooded slopes, a little above and away from the sea, providing the best collection of *cottages ornés* in the country.

Sidmouth has retained its *recherché* atmosphere to this day, when many other Regency resorts have become tattered at the edges. Its safe distance from London played a part in keeping Victorian day-trippers at bay, and its dramatic setting prevented a suburban sprawl.

The Grand Duchess Helen of Russia took a house on the esplanade in 1818, and the Duke and Duchess of Kent with their baby daughter, Princess Victoria, the future queen, took Woolbrook Cottage (now the Royal Glen Hotel) in 1819. In 1820 a cricket field was laid out near the middle of the town. Nowhere could top Sidmouth. Sir John Soane built Knowle Cottage (which today has been utterly changed) for Lord Despenser, and remarkable *cottages ornés* continued to spring up right through the nineteenth century. This Sidmouth seaside style reached a peak of fancifulness when, in 1856, a Mr Johnstone bought Woodlands Cottage, tastefully Gothicised by Lord Gwydir, and proceeded to lavish it with appendages. He replaced the thatch with hexagonal slates and embellished the dormers with stone icing-sugar barge-boards painted pink, prepared in Italy and shipped to England. Sidmouth had gone about as far as it could in social and architectural terms. Johnstone's barge-boards were thought to be rather vulgar by the aristocracy who still spent their summers under Sidmouth's sky, but in the end the call of Nice and Monte Carlo was stronger than the sploshing of waves on the shingle of Jacob's Ladder beach. They left, leaving their wonderful architecture behind them.

Left: Sidmouth from Peak Hill

Sledmere, Yorkshire

The wide chalk uplands of the Wolds are crossed by open roads edged with wind-bent hedges, giving views to bare, sweeping horizons and glimpses of distant blue country. Sometimes there are long dark woods and coppices, half-hidden in hollows, or small villages set in shallow valleys lying low against the ever-bracing winds. If there are clouds, more often than not they are scudding fast, but on some days a sea fret comes in from the coast and obliterates every feature with a thick mist.

'Sledmere may be considered the ornament of that bleak hilly country,' wrote the author John Bigland in 1812. 'In summer the waving crops in the fields, the houses of the tenantry elegantly constructed, the numerous and extensive plantations skirting the slope of the hills and the superb mansion with its ornamental ground in the centre of the vale form a magnificent and luxuriant assemblage...' Over 150 years later Sledmere still shines out as an exemplary kingdom, well loved and well cared for.

The village itself sits in a shallow dip in the hills. Along its main street, past farm and stud buildings, richly detailed Victorian estate houses and cottages line one side of the road, all built of the local gingery-red brick and adorned with deep barge boards and grand rainwater hoppers bearing *fleurs-de-lis* designs. Before them kempt gardens are half hidden by neatly clipped holly hedges above low brick walls. The postbox, set in the leaded lattice window of the Post Office, still bears the letters 'GR'. On past the creeper-clad eighteenth-century rectory stands a dignified domed rotunda raised on columns above a well. It was built in memory of Sir Christopher Sykes, 'who by his assiduity and perseverance,' the inscription reads, 'in building and planting and inclosing on the Yorkshire Wolds, in the short space of thirty years, set such an example to the other owners of the land, as has caused what once was a bleak and barren tract of country to become now one of the most productive and best cultivated districts in the county of York.'

Across the road, lodges and grand gates herald the entrance to the park, which curves and sweeps gently away up to the Sykes of Sledmere's elegant house, with its faintly raised eyebrows arched over the windows. Spectacular beech trees around it look anchored to the ground by their huge spreading skirts, up to eighty feet across. Each generation of Sykes has planted trees so there is a never-ending succession to come. Richard Sykes laid the foundation stone for the house in 1751 and planted twenty thousand trees, but his son Christopher had far more grandiose schemes. First he employed Thomas White and subsequently Capability Brown to lay out pleasure grounds and rides and to draw up proposals for improvements. By 1779 he had planted 177,210 trees – mostly beech, Scots pine and larch. He built strategically placed farms and other buildings – eye-catchers at the end of wooded views to be seen from the house, like the mile-distant and castellated Castle Farm (by John Carr of York). As if the Wolds had not been justly rewarded by Christopher's planting, his grandson Tatton became even more of a legend. He restored or built afresh sixteen churches in the neighbourhood, and according to Gordon Home, writing on Yorkshire in 1908, Tatton was 'the sort of man that Yorkshire folk came near to worshipping. He was of that hearty, genial, conservative type that filled the hearts of the farmers with pride. On market days all over the Riding one of the always fresh subjects of conversation was how Sir Tatton was looking. So great was the conservatism of this remarkable squire that years after the advent of railways he continued to make his journey to Epsom, for the Derby, on horseback.'

Right: Sledmere House
Inset: the Sykes of Sledmere have long loved bull terriers

Right: the Soane Museum
Inset: the museum
houses Soane's vast
collection of antiquities

Sir John Soane's Museum, **London**

An air of strict legality hovers above the plane trees in the central gardens of Lincoln's Inn Fields. The houses around it are reserved – until, that is, you notice Sir John Soane's former home. The strange facade was originally designed as a loggia, which Soane later filled in with windows to give extra space within. The architect of the Bank of England and the Dulwich Art Gallery, he left his house to the nation.

Soane was a genius. His architecture was miles ahead of its time and annoyed the purists. It combined a slow-arched elegance with amazingly modern ideas, such as recycling the wasted heat from chimneys through the passages of a house. The son of an Essex bricklayer, he was born in Goring-on-Thames and started his life as an errand boy. He entered the office of the architect George Dance the Younger and later of Henry Holland. His talent at drawing was soon recognised. He won the Royal Academy Gold Medal for a design of a triumphal bridge. Sir William Chambers saw it and introduced him to George III, and his career began its meteoric rise. His house in Lincoln's Inn Fields, which he combined as a home, a studio and a gallery, encapsulates his brilliance.

The Sir John Soane Museum, as his house is now called, does not display the modern spareness of many of his country houses but instead contains more ingenious design ideas than it is possible to imagine. Soane first moved to Number 12 in 1792 and, having added Numbers 13 and 14 to make a single house, proceeded over the next forty-five years to embellish it with every architectural trick he knew.

As soon as you venture through the front door you lose all sense of orientation. Nothing is normal. The use of space is quite extraordinary. The dining-room, which is combined with the library, has mirrored arches and shutters and circles above the books. The reflections are endless, optically illusive and, by candlelight, dazzling. The whole place is beautifully cared for and even on a dull day the fire irons and fenders, the furniture and worn leather seats glisten from their weekly polishings. It's a man's room, painted Pompeiian red and bronzed green, as is the little study and dressing-room directly off it, which is like a ship's cabin with not an inch wasted.

The breakfast-room is my favourite room in the house, with its domed ceiling and inset mirrors which give it a sparkling brilliance, but it is satisfactorily practical as well. The picture room, where you can see Hogarth's *The Rake's Progress*, has huge and surprising swinging panels housing more pictures than you would think possible in so small a space. There are optically elusive corridors of Corinthian columns, and crypts beneath which were once the backyards of the houses. The custodians refer to them as the 'Valley of Death' since they contain so many remnants of Greek tombs and a gigantic Egyptian sarcophagus. Although Soane was purported to be a depressive, the upstairs drawing-rooms could not be merrier. They are painted in the most wonderful 'patent' yellow with stiff silk curtains to match, and when the sun shines through the stained glass on the sides of the glazed-in loggia you might easily be in the South of France. Soane was an obsessive collector. He scanned every catalogue and haunted the salesrooms. He did not always go to the auctions, but Mrs Soane, a considerable heiress, often did and it was she who bid for *The Rake's Progress* at Christie's in 1802 and secured the eight canvasses for £570. The house is stuffed with *objets d'art*, architectural models, drawings and paintings (including Turners), all arranged in an inimitable and intimate way. It is not at all like a museum – just a wonderful private house belonging to an extraordinary man.

Somersby, Lincolnshire

A mild sea fret had come in from the coast as I came into Salmonby, but I could still see the soft woods falling away into the folds of the hills. The country between here and Somersby is some of the prettiest in England. The scale of the Lincolnshire Wolds is cosier than those of Yorkshire and the roads far emptier. Chestnut trees towered from the hedges along the roadside as I neared the village. It is a quiet place, little changed, and tucked into a gentle fold with the eastern ridge of the Wolds at its back and the broad meadows before it, stretching away and disappearing towards the sea. Somersby had always been a backwater until 1808, when the Reverend George Tennyson came there as rector of St Margaret's Church and also of the church of Bag Enderby just down the road. He arrived a disappointed man. His father had not approved of his marriage to Miss Fytche of Louth and had disinherited him in favour of his younger brother Charles, who consequently came into the family estate of Bayons Manor near Tealby.

George was forced to take Holy Orders, and throughout his life found the calling a burden. He and his wife already had a son, Frederick, when they came to the village, but they proceeded to have a further ten children, including Charles and Alfred, both future poets, who were born in 1808 and 1809 respectively. The Tennysons were a family of poets, for Alfred's father wrote good verse and his paternal grandmother claimed that all the poetry in the family came through her. Some undeniably came through Somersby.

The lane curls into the village past high hedges of may and billows of cow parsley spilling from the banks across the brook immortalised in 'In Memoriam' – 'On yon swoll'n brook that bubbles fast / By meadows breathing of the past.' The Rectory where the Tennysons lived is plain-faced, cream-painted Georgian, with pantile roofs. To this, Alfred's father added a large Gothic dining-room on the garden side, built for him by his coachman, Horlins. In those days the rest of the house contained narrow passages and many tiny rooms. Behind the Rectory was a beautiful garden which gave onto open country.

And one an English home — gray twilight pour'd
On dewy pastures, dewy trees,
Softer than sleep — all things in order stored,
A haunt of ancient Peace.

Next to the Rectory, in this haunt of ancient peace, is the rarefied early eighteenth-century Grange, built of red-brick with arched windows and castellations like a miniature fort.

Across the way is the little medieval church of St Margaret's, built of brick-patched greenstone and containing a handsome bust of the Poet Laureate himself, together with a small case full of souvenirs and mementoes. At Somersby the spirit of Alfred Tennyson is all-pervading, as is the rural peace into which he was born and which he knew so well. In 1837 the Tennyson family left the Rectory.

We leave the well-beloved place
Where first we gazed upon the sky;
The roofs that heard our earliest cry
Will shelter one of stranger race.

But still, leaving Somersby and travelling the deep-cut lane to Bag Enderby, the poetry of Tennyson is everywhere. It is here in the greenstone church, grander and more beautiful than Somersby's, and in this peaceful, tiny cul-de-sac of farm and school and chestnut trees. It is here in this valley as you pass nearby Harrington Hall, a fine brick mansion with a projecting porch, once the home of Rosa Baring with whom Tennyson was hopelessly in love. Here are the terraced gardens about which he wrote in 'Maud':

Birds in the high Hall-garden
When twilight was falling,
Maud, Maud, Maud, Maud,
They were crying and calling.

Far left: Somersby Rectory, where Alfred Tennyson was born in 1809

Southend-on-Sea, Essex

The train from London cuts through Limehouse, Barking and Upminster and then strikes out into low, lost, unsung Thames-side Essex. From West Horndon, Laindon and Basildon, the train speeds on to muddier and marshier Pitsea and Benfleet. To the south you can see the eerie island of Canvey where one night in 1953 a storm swept through and fifty-eight people were drowned. Scattered with bungalows and chalets, it is now guarded by floodgates and a massive concrete sea-wall.

At Leigh-on-Sea, there are cockle, mussel, whelk and jellied eel stalls on the mud flats between the train and the estuary. High above the old fishing village, with its Crooked Billet Inn and its High Street leading down to the shore, stands the church of St Clement. All is surrounded by nineteenth-century development in what is today a suburb of Southend, as are the next two stops – Chalkwell and Westcliff.

When you get out at Southend station and start the short walk down the bustling High Street towards the water's edge, and see the longest pier in the world venturing out into the Thames Estuary, you can't help feeling you're on holiday. The change from London's serious atmosphere to the frivolous gaiety of Southend is total. Whatever the weather – and I usually come here in the winter months – the sea front is dedicated to pure pleasure. It is also beautiful. You would never guess that gregarious Southend has its roots in a twelfth-century priory in what was one of Essex's oldest villages, Prittlewell. From Priory Crescent, a path leads across Priory Park to the Clunic remains of church, cloisters, refectory and living quarters. A thriving community of oyster fishermen had grown up around the priory at its southern end – hence the name Southend. Following the Dissolution of the monasteries, some of the buildings were converted into a house and the church was pulled down. Over the succeeding centuries the house was enlarged and given a Georgian facade. Following the First World War, it was presented to the Corporation of Southend and is now the Borough Museum.

The first attempts to transform Southend into a holiday resort began at the end of the eighteenth century. Entrepreneurial developers, cashing in on people's hypochondriacal fixation with their health, were alighting on likely sites all around England's coast. But Southend was slow to catch on compared to Margate and Brighton. Princess Caroline of Wales and her daughter Charlotte both stayed here at the very beginning of the nineteenth century and the new resort became briefly fashionable – Regency terraces were built up on the esplanade above the sea, as well as a grand stucco hotel which gained the title of 'Royal' after the princess's visit. However, by the 1820s the aristocracy had already deserted Southend and, although it retained a quieter, posher end around Thorpe Bay (still the smart place to live), it was the coming of the railway in the 1850s and the creation of Bank Holidays in 1870 that brought a different kind of success – hordes of day-trippers from London. London's East Enders could be by the seaside in under an hour. Southend's clamorous cockle-stall reputation began.

The hub of the resort, Marine Parade, gradually filled up with public houses, slot machines, amusement arcades and bingo halls. Playgrounds and funfairs abounded, and the town spread ever outwards to Shoeburyness and Benfleet around over a thousand acres of parks.

Despite its present size, Southend is still elegant and still exciting. The pier stretches for nearly a mile and a half. In 1939 the Royal Navy took it over and renamed it HMS *Leigh*. It became an operations centre and an assembly point from which nearly 3,500 convoys sailed. A railway running along the promenade deck the length of the pier carried the sick and wounded in one direction and supplies in the other. Today you can still take the train to the end of the pier and sit, watching gigantic ships sail by.

Right: Southend pier, built in 1830, is the longest pleasure pier in the world at 1.33 miles long

Southport, **Merseyside**

Southport is a classy place. Facing out across an enormous inland lake which looks towards the Irish Sea, it trails along on the sandy edge of the low-lying Mosses, as they call them here. Once mudflats, salt marsh, swamp and mere spreading twenty miles inland, they were, like the eastern Fens and the Somerset Levels, well drained with dykes and ditches by the Dutch.

At the end of the eighteenth century *recherché* villas and houses began to be built among the sand hills ('hawes' or 'meols' to Lancastrians). The local landowners, Madam Bold of Bold and her nephew Bold Fleetwood Hesketh, granted leases to speculators prohibiting the building of factories. A planning principle was soon established according to which the town developed over the next century and the restrictions enforced made for a conspicuous absence of slums. There were never any telegraph or electricity poles in the town – all were buried from the start. Almost every house, however small, had a front and back garden. In effect Southport was the first garden city in the country.

In 1825 an Act of Parliament obtained by the Fleetwood Hesketh family made a proviso that Lord Street, Southport's showpiece, should be eighty-eight yards wide. Today its level one-and-a-half-mile length running parallel to the sea, with wide tree-shaded pavements, makes you feel you are walking down some foreign boulevard. A handsome and continuous glass-topped wrought-iron veranda stretches out in front of the shops along much of Lord Street's west side. Coloured lights smother the trees at night and Victorian church spires, a campanile and a great obelisk rise up from leafy streets to the east. Napoleon III was said to be so impressed by the scale of Lord Street when he visited Southport that his layout of nineteenth-century Paris may well have been influenced by it.

Although the six-mile stretch of sandy beach is only covered by the sea at spring tides, when it sweeps in at the speed of a galloping horse, this elegant resort has always been a desirable place to live. In Birkdale on the south side of town, Southport's poshest suburb and family home of historian A J P Taylor, Liverpool and Everton football players and their WAGs lurk behind electronic gates in sumptuous red-brick Victorian villas with billiard-table lawns mown in diagonal stripes. On the north side, Hesketh Park contains both a meteorological and an astronomical observatory. Serpentine paths weave between high 'meols', clumps of Scots pines, flashy flowerbeds and out past a 'Tudor' lodge into quiet streets of Edwardian houses whose front gardens are full of almond blossom, amelanchier and clipped laurels.

At Churchtown a sudden clutch of thatched cottages, two ancient inns and a church around a little square are what remains of the original village from which the seed of Southport sprang. An innkeeper called William Sutton used some driftwood from the beach to build the first bathing house of all. Nearby are the gates to Meols Hall, still the home of the Hesketh family, the enlightened planners of Southport. The Moss spreads away towards the distant Pennines.

Large crowds may flock to Southport's famous flower and horse shows, and to the Ryder Cup when it is held at the Royal Birkdale Golf Club, but over ten thousand people visit the British Lawnmower Museum on the first floor above Stanley's Discount Garden Machinery Warehouse every year. Started by Southport-born Brian Radam, who served as an apprentice at garden machinery company Atco and went on to become a champion lawnmower racer, it displays over two hundred machines from the first solar-powered robot-mower to the fastest lawnmower ever made. There are rows of discarded lawnmowers of the 'rich and famous' including those of the Prince of Wales, Alan Titchmarsh, Nicholas Parsons, and the little-push cylinder mower which belonged to *Coronation Street*'s Hilda Ogden.

Right: Lord Street in Southport with its glass-topped wrought-iron veranda

Southwell, **Nottinghamshire**

Nottinghamshire remains relatively unnoticed and unappreciated by travellers speeding through it on the M1 or the train. Though it is revered by cricketers for its hallowed ground at Trent Bridge, and romantically lodged in our imaginations thanks to Robin Hood, it has never been on the tourist trail. Factories and pit heads, power stations and pylons have sprouted amidst farms and villages, mild manors and ducal estates. D H Lawrence, Nottinghamshire's famous son, accused the Victorian promoters of industry of condemning workers to '...ugliness, ugliness, ugliness: meaningless and formless and ugly surroundings, ugly ideals, ugly religion, ugly hope, ugly love, ugly furniture, ugly houses ... The human soul needs actual beauty even more than bread.' But this stalwart, unselfconscious county is full of hidden beauty. Take Southwell for instance – there could be no more perfect small town in all England.

The road from Nottingham runs alongside the valley of the mighty Trent through red-brick villages and pretty farming country of small hills and pastureland. From miles away, you can see Southwell Minster, the mother church of Nottinghamshire rising from the small hill town, like a large ship sailing above a sea of roofs. For nine hundred years it was the domain of the Archbishops of York, who founded the college of secular canons here and who were responsible for all the buildings. It was only in 1884 that Southwell became a separate see.

The Minster stands in wide sweeps of greensward scattered with gravestones and studded with primroses in spring. The Bishop's manor and ruins of the Archbishop's Palace border one side of the green, the handsome red-brick Vicar's Court another, and Westgate and Church Street, full of elegant Georgian and Regency architecture, including several ravishing prebendal houses, enclose the remainder. There is a peaceful air.

The Minster is not daunting. Its scale is friendly, but its beauty is overwhelming. From the west it still looks the same as it did when the Normans first built it in the 1100s, with its French-looking conical hats on top of the towers. (Although rebuilt, they replicate what was there before.) Once through the great oak doors carved with latticework and into the cool calm of the Romanesque nave, Patrick Reyntiens's magnificent new stained-glass window cannot fail to draw your eye west. It depicts hosts of angels and archangels and lifts the heart. When I visited, the afternoon sun struck shafts of light through all the south windows and lit the golden stone all through the Minster as though it were part of it. The place was almost empty and completely silent.

I stayed in the small octagonal chapter house for a long time. Decorating the gables, capitals, spandrels and crockets of the thirty-six stalls which line the walls, 'The Leaves of Southwell' are justly celebrated. Hawthorn, oak, maple, hop, white bryony, vine, ivy, apple rose and buttercup leaves retain the crisp perfection of the day they were carved in the thirteenth century. They are the leaves of our countryside and their simple freshness is moving beyond compare.

Southwell is an elegant and pleasing town. The half-timbered Saracen's Head on Westgate, where Charles I spent his last night as a free man, is quirkily romantic, the market square pocket-sized, King Street just the right scale to shop in, Burnham Grange famous for Byron's visits when his mum lived there. But it's the ancient apple tree in a cottage garden at the eastern end of town that is the prize exhibit. Mr Bramley planted a pip in a pot in 1805 and forty years later a local nursery man asked if he could take cuttings from it. Bramley agreed on condition his name was attached to what became our favourite cooking apple.

Right: Southwell Minster

Stamford, Lincolnshire

The beauty of Stamford is hard to beat. If you stand on Town Meadows, sandwiched between two branches of the River Welland, the view of church towers and spires sailing above Stamford's rooftops is magical. The town is all built of the same mellow limestone which gives it a head start in the beauty stakes but it also seems to have remained untouched by urban blight. This partly dates back to William Cecil, a local man who became Queen Elizabeth I's Secretary of State and was granted the manor of Stamford under her reign. He built the palatial pile of Burghley for his mother close by and his family have been politically and financially involved with the town ever since.

From the Meadows a footbridge leads across the river to The George. To have tea here by a big log fire on a Friday afternoon in winter is a recipe for perfect contentment. Toasted tea cakes, slices of Lincolnshire plum loaf, glimpses across the tea tables to further panelled rooms on higgledy-piggledy levels and through the window to a cobbled courtyard behind, the beamed ceiling above and a grandfather clock ticking in the corner add to the settled and reassuring comfort of the place. There is a quiet and almost hallowed sense of occasion in the air. I think it is the done thing for the Lincolnshire well-to-do to come to The George for tea after shopping in the Shambles on market day. In the hall there is a portrait of Daniel Lambert, renowned in his lifetime for being England's fattest man. He died in Stamford in 1809 weighing fifty-three stone and is buried in St Mary's churchyard.

For a thousand years there has been a hostelry standing here on the Great North Road near Town Bridge (which replaced Stamford's original 'ford'). Once owned by the Abbots of Croyland, the old coaching inn tells the story of the town's development from its prominence as a trading place to its first ecclesiastical flowering in the thirteenth century. Three great churches were built and religious houses began to proliferate, two of which now form part of The George. Dominicans, Carmelites, Austin Friars and Franciscans founded monastic institutions, friaries, schools and colleges, and Stamford's reputation as a seat of learning grew so much that it attracted a splinter group of dissatisfied Oxford academics. For a short time during the fourteenth century they established a break-away university in what was by then one of the ten largest towns in England.

The Wars of the Roses took their toll on Yorkist Stamford. The Lancastrians sacked and burnt much of it, and the general prosperity of the townspeople through wool-trading, the making of worsteds and pottery declined. Only a few rich merchants got richer and as a result built more churches and almshouses. Because of improved road conditions, the traffic through Stamford multiplied during the eighteenth century and most people travelling north or south stopped here. The George expanded accordingly and Stamford's social life thrived around the newly built Assembly Rooms and theatre. Handsome townhouses sprang up on every street and it is their elegance and sheer quantity which make Stamford unique. The opening of the railway line to the north in 1844 meant that the town was bypassed. Victorian expansion and industrialisation never came.

Although the coaching trade petered out, The George survived as an integral part of the perfectly-sized market town Stamford is today. After tea, if you dip into the quietude of the second-hand bookshop in an ancient building on St Mary Hill and gaze at the first editions behind locked glass doors, you might just feel the haunting presence of those revolutionary Oxford academics looking over your shoulder.

Right: across the bridge towards St Mary's Church in Stamford

Stanhope, County Durham

Over Bollihope Common there is eyebright in the sheep-cropped turf beside the road to Stanhope. A lone lady bicyclist with nut-brown legs glides effortlessly towards me, up to the brow of the hill after her steady four-mile climb. Across the peaty-watered Bollihope Burn, where a Roman altar was discovered in 1747, the road becomes alarmingly steep and hairpins down Quarry Hill towards this loveliest of open, wooded valleys, hiding the River Wear below. Huge scoops have been sculpted out of the hills thanks to old quarry workings. Grassed over now, they have become like giant works of abstract art. There are two sturdy-looking black Dales ponies looking over the stone wall beside the road, their ears pricked, their shoulders enormously strong. Years ago Dales were used to carry coal in panniers from the mines to the towns. Once they knew the route they would make the journey on their own, unsupervised. There are patches of thistles in the rabbit-hold pasture, which falls away to the small town of Stanhope.

The white cottage and old level-crossing of the Wear Valley Railway are signs of Stanhope's important industrial past. Just beyond is a lyrically beautiful raggle-taggle farm where black hens scratch around elder bushes in the yard. Beside it is the most ravishing ancient and jumbled pale limestone house called Unthank Hall, with mullioned windows, lichened stone-tiled roofs and ivy- and valerian-covered garden walls. The air of faint dishevelment enhances the beauty of the place. The Madison family began to build it in the fifteenth century when the local lead mines were prosperous beyond compare, and Stanhope grew in stature to become a market town. The tithes from the lead mines rendered Stanhope's the wealthiest living in England, and as a result produced many eminent rectors, eight of whom became Bishops, including Bishop Butler of Durham.

Beyond Unthank is a wide, shallow ford across the River Wear, dark in the shade of sycamores. There are stepping-stones for walkers, and on the far side a leafy lane turns down into Stanhope, along its one and only main street, Front Street. Grey- or buff-stoned and slate-roofed houses line the way. It is a plain, strong-feeling, unpretentious town with a rough industrial edge – a welcome contrast to some of the overtly and self-consciously pretty villages of the more tourist-trailed Dales. The 1903 town hall is suitably gloomy, the unchained shops make you feel happy and at home, and the farmer's market prospers.

By the Pack Horse Inn, the small market square is cobbled and calm. Beside it are the faintly sinister castellated heights of Stanhope Castle, built as a flight of fancy in the late-eighteenth century for Cuthbert Rippon, the MP for Gateshead. It was enlarged in a heavy-handed manner by the Victorians in order to house both a collection of stuffed birds and a large number of shooting guests. By the middle of the twentieth century the Castle had become a remand home. The solid squat-towered church across the way harbours, in its dark interior, the Roman altar from Bollihope inscribed to Silvanus, the god of the countryside associated in particular with woods. The hills around Stanhope have always been hung with woods. The fossilised tree stump at the churchyard gate is a quarter of a million years old.

With nineteenth-century Stanhope's success through the mining of lead, lime and ore, as well as through the iron works and the gas and light company, came solid Victorian munificence and spiritual guidance. Methodist and Wesleyan chapels sprang up as well as church schools, provision for the poor and solid civic buildings. Along Front Street the Victorians have certainly left their mark, but on the steep lane leading out of the town's wooded valley towards the moorland heights and Northumberland, Stanhope Old Hall, a great medieval jumble of a place, serves as a reminder of the town's early days. Up on the common above, and all around it, the traces of ancient mine workings all bear witness to the town's strong pioneering spirit and its lucrative first beginnings.

Right: the Pack Horse Inn

Stanway, Gloucestershire

I know of no more beautiful group of buildings than Stanway's. They are set on a Pilgrim's or 'stony' way (hence its name) which wends its way southwards for a mile or so to the ruined abbey of Hailes and then on up into the wooded slopes of the great Cotswold escarpment. Stanway's ancient and settled feel is absolute and although its buildings have evolved over a thousand years, they form a glorious and golden whole. The church, fourteenth-century tithe barn, Jacobean gatehouse, Victorian stable block and gabled manor-house are all built of the same golden limestone from the Jackdaw Quarry high on the hill above.

The original Stanway Manor was granted to the abbots of Tewkesbury in AD 715 by two rich Mercian brothers called Odo and Dodo. Even before this county came to house more abbeys than any other in England (provoking the saying 'As sure as God's in Gloucestershire'), four monks were already residing here in a cell. The monastic settlement grew over the next seven hundred years and by the sixteenth century the covetous Tracy family of nearby Toddington had spotted the property development potential of Stanway. The Tracys were directly descended from one of the four knights who murdered Thomas à Becket and their infamy among the locals was legendary – 'The Tracys, the Tracys, the wind in their faces,' they used to say as the Tracys fled the ghosts and curses of their past. They ingratiated themselves with Thomas Cromwell, promoted the dissolution of Stanway by telling awful stories about it, and attained a lease in 1533. It was one of the earliest monastic settlements to be dissolved by Henry VIII. Richard Tracy subsequently led the commission which dissolved Hailes, declared its sacred phial of the Holy Blood to be duck's blood tinted with saffron, and took part in the dismantling of the building.

The wind changed when the enlightened Charteris family married into the Tracy line. Today the house's atmosphere remains predominantly Stuart, despite the fact that it has been added to and changed over the centuries. The oriel window of the hall, with over a thousand leaded lights, floods the west side of the house with evening light. Cynthia Charteris, later Asquith, who was born here in 1887, referred to the window in her diaries 'as so mellowed by time that whenever the sun shines through their amber and green glass, the effect is of a vast honeycomb and indeed at all times and in all weathers of stored sunshine.'

Her mother Mary Wyndham, who married the eldest Charteris son Lord Elcho, brought a certain fame to Stanway by becoming a member of 'The Souls', a risqué circle of rich aristocrats who met regularly to discuss 'higher things'. Albeit absentmindedly, she ruled the roost at Stanway and was happy to condone the local vicar's eccentric promotion of free love and whisky drinking.

The present Charteris descendant has long been restoring the elaborate water garden, which had fallen into a crumbling state of disrepair. Originally created in the 1720s on the dramatically steep hill behind the house, it comprised an ornamental canal on a levelled terrace twenty-five feet above and a stepped cascade falling down into it from a pyramid-shaped temple. A few years ago, when the local authority decided to abandon an enormous reservoir 530 feet up in the heights of Lidcombe Wood because the water had been contaminated by sheep, the idea for a spectacular fountain was conceived. The power engendered from the fall of water, fed down a polythene pipe into a two-inch bronze nozzle into the ornamental canal, was enough to shoot a plume of water three hundred feet into the sky. It reigns supreme as the highest gravity-fed fountain in the world.

Far left: Stanway Manor
Inset: the oriel window
in the hall

Swinbrook and Widford, Oxfordshire

A mile downstream from Burford, the Windrush Valley opens out around the lost village of Widford, now just a tiny hamlet. You can cross the bridge by the old mill and take the dead-end lane which leads up to the mullion-windowed manor. Just below it, past a wide reedy pond, you follow the north bank of the Windrush towards Swinbrook, by way of Widford's tiny church of St Oswald. It sits remote in sheep pasture crossed by silvery stone walls in all directions. Around it is the undulating ground where once a thriving village stood with two working mills. Built on the foundations of a Roman villa, the barn-like church – derelict in the nineteenth century – was beautifully restored at the beginning of the next and its wall paintings revealed. An ancient and sacred atmosphere prevails and it is worth every step of the sheep-scattered way to enter and sit for a while in one of its simple box pews. On down the valley, the village of Swinbrook unfurls in grey-gold Cotswold stone, and the lane leads past farmhouses and Victorian lattice-windowed cottages to the church of St Mary. To its south and south-west is the site of what was once one of the greatest houses in Oxfordshire and the home for centuries of the extravagantly rich-from-wool family of Fettiplace. Though the vestiges of their mansion may be only grassy mounds, their monuments inside the church, beside the huge clear glass window which fills the whole of the east end and floods the place with light, are so magnificent you will never forget them. Three Tudor Fettiplaces, for want of space in the chancel, lie sandwiched, stiff, startled and haughty in their armour on an elegant three-tiered bunk bed, resting their heads on their right arms and their elbows on cushions. They stare alarmingly into space. Beside them in a Stuart bunk bed lie a later lot in more casual and cavalier poses with knees bent. They look marginally more comfortable.

When the Fettiplace line had petered out, their mansion was let in 1806 to a Mr Freeman of London. 'References were waived,' read the *Oxford Magazine*, 'in consideration of his pleasant habit of paying down unending guineas in advance when asked for security.' He came equipped with an army of servants, was an

immediate hit in the neighbourhood and dined in every stately home around. Soon after his arrival, the area was terrorised by a spate of highway robberies and for a year or more no one thought to suspect the Freeman household until the butler was shot dead in a robbery and identified.

Outside in the churchyard lie four of the five legendary Mitford sisters, including Nancy, whose novel *The Pursuit of Love* is set in Swinbrook ('Alconleigh'), their childhood home. There is a simple plaque in the church to the memory of their brother, Thomas, who was killed in action in Burma in 1945.

In 1919 their eccentric father, Lord Redesdale, bought Asthall Manor, one village down the Windrush, but found it so haunted (the cook's bedclothes were pulled off almost nightly by a ghost) that he sold it and moved to Swinbrook, where he enlarged and aggrandised a farmhouse. He put in new elm doors which warped so badly that the bathrooms afforded no privacy whatsoever. At the bottom of the village a gaggle of geese graze the meadow across from The Swan Inn and the disused mill. A clear slice of the river still hurtles violently through, wisteria climbs thickly about and a fat holly leans on the inn walls.

Right: St Mary's Church in Swinbrook

Tissington, Derbyshire

Above Dove Dale, so sung by Izaak Walton in *The Compleat Angler*, and on beside blossomy may trees edging the ridge and furrow fields, Tissington lies in a fold, hidden from the world. Great gate piers on the Buxton to Ashbourne road herald the public way, which leads gently down an avenue of young limes and into the village.

It is an exceptionally beautiful place. It has the feeling that no planner or bossy nannying bureaucrat has ever been near it. There are no road signs and no lampposts. It has grown haphazardly and effortlessly around a gentle bowl of land. Many of the houses and cottages, built of the palest damson stone with whiter stone dressings around the windows, have little walled gardens in front of them. When I visited in late May, they were gay with tulips, aubretia, wallflowers, valerian and occasional lines of washing. Sheepdogs barked at a gate beside a stately Irish yew.

From the village pond the road winds up a gentle slope bordered by wide sweeping grass verges. A three-storeyed ivy-clad farmhouse stands next to the church of St Mary, squat and ancient on the brow of a small hill. The Norman tower has four-foot thick walls, and inside there is a wonderful font decorated with primitive carvings of dragon-like beasts with tails curling round their bodies, and Henry Moore-like people standing around. There is an exceptionally showy lopsided monument on the simple chancel arch, built to the memory of Francis Fitzherbert (d 1619) and to his son John. The Fitzherbert family, who still live in the manor-house today and still own the village, had come into it through a chain of medieval heiresses. Since then the history of the village has been inextricably woven with theirs.

On up the street, just north of the church, cattle graze on grassy tumps and mounds – the romantic remains of a Derbyshire hill fort and the site of the old hall. Francis Fitzherbert, however, preferred to live on the sunny side of the street and at the beginning of the seventeenth century set about building his house directly opposite. There it stands in its plain Jacobean symmetry, right in the middle of things. It is approached through an arched gateway in the garden wall which runs along the street. Since then, various Fitzherberts have added onto the simple core in erratic and decidedly asymmetrical fashion so that the house is now eccentrically jumbled but friendly, and feels very much part of the village, hugger-mugger with its neighbours.

The Fitzherberts, rich through their sugar plantations in Barbados and Jamaica, as well as through the slave trade while it existed, could afford to be philanthropic. During the middle of the nineteenth century, ever dutiful towards the well-being of the villagers, Sir Henry and his sister became indefatigable builders. They commissioned many of the handsome cottages, the school and a side-aisle to the church in the Norman style. The Arts and Crafts village hall at the bottom of the hill near the pond, built by a later Fitzherbert, is exceptional.

Tissington is particularly proud of its long tradition of well dressing, an ancient custom which is virtually peculiar to Derbyshire. Around the five village wells – Hall Well, Hands Well, Coffin Well, Town Well and Yew Tree Well – the villagers depict biblical scenes by sticking myriad flower petals like mosaics into boards of wet clay in time for Ascension Day. Although purportedly a pagan ritual, it was revived by Christians as a way of thanking God for the purity of the water supply. Tissington's wells have never run dry and are said to have saved its villagers from contracting the Black Death. Nothing could have saved the unlucky villager, James Allsop, however. His gravestone relates he was 'drownded' in the *Titanic* disaster of 1912.

Left: the village hall beyond the pond with the manor in the background
Inset: traditional well dressing at Tissington

Torquay, **Devon**

'Torquay is a magic town built of high harbour walls and shining palaces beside the sea,' wrote Nevil Shute in *Lonely Road*. Today, you only have to blur your vision a little, obscuring the odd 1960s block towering awkwardly among the elegant stucco housing, and the magic is still there. Down past the big hotels in Belgrave Road, swags of coloured lights – blue, gold, green, white and red – stretch between the lampposts all along the seafront, illuminating the Regina Hotel with its elaborate wrought-iron balconies, the Princess Theatre, where *We'll Meet Again – Hits from the Blitz* is playing, the jaunty Edwardian pavilion, patterned with green and white tiles, bandstands on its corners, fountains in its wake, and the harbour full of sailing boats which boasts a most exotic aquarium.

Torquay lies on one of the most beautiful stretches of the English Riviera, in the warm, balmy shelter of Torbay, between Hope's Nose and Berry Head, remnants of a great barrier reef. It's a good place to visit at the back end of the year when the rain is slashing sideways and the winter blues have set in. I walked down to Meadfoot Bay in the evening. The path zigzags through kempt, palmy gardens from the grandest Regency crescent I ever saw, its long slow curve shining white above the sea. Precipitous, hanging woods cling to the hillside all around – Scots pine, ilex and oak sweeping dramatically from sky to shoreline – and the lights of Brixham began to shine across the bay.

The spectacular terrain is the dominant feature of the town. If you stand on Warren Road and look down towards the bay you will see that two-thirds of the steep hills and canyon-like valleys of Torquay are taken up with great shoulders of rock or lush canopies of trees – planes, beeches, macrocarpa, cedars and palm trees. Striking between are steep, winding roads from which drives lead off to Italianate villas half hidden by lush gardens stuffed with hydrangeas and fuchsias. Twenty-three churches and chapels call holiday-makers to God and Victorian spires strike up against the hillsides. A grey stone town hall promotes the holiday atmosphere. Carved large on its walls are quotes by Addison and Izaak Walton respectively: 'Health and cheerfulness mutually beget each other' and 'Good company and good discourse are the very sinews of virtue.' Lions' heads, holding what appear to be doughnuts in their mouths, look down from above.

High on a hill is Kent's Cavern, where remnants of Stone Age man and the bones of extinct animals were discovered by the Victorians, and down towards the sea are the remains of the twelfth-century Torre Abbey, its gatehouse, abbot's tower and magnificent tithe barn. As the Abbey grew richer, the monks built a small quay below and a tiny fishing hamlet evolved – Torquay. It remained a relatively quiet backwater until the arrival of the Channel fleet. By the early nineteenth century it became a minor watering centre and a haven for the families of naval officers and their sweethearts during the Napoleonic wars. Rich invalids began to visit Torquay for its mild, soothing climate and invigorating sea air.

With the opening of the railway in 1848 Torquay was promoted still further, and grand terraces and crescents sprang up, prompting Walter Savage Landor to comment, 'Torquay is full of smart ugly houses, and rich hot-looking people.' By the beginning of the twentieth century its respectability was so stifling that on visiting the town Rudyard Kipling exclaimed, 'I do desire to upset it by dancing through it with nothing on but my spectacles. Villas, clipped hedges, and shaven lawns, fat ladies with respirators...'

183

Tregardock Cliffs, Cornwall

Tregardock Cliffs are terrifying, inhospitable and tremendous. They lie on the windswept eastern side of the parish of St Teath (pronounced to rhyme with death), where only a few scattered farms hang well back from the edge and brave the sea gales. This particular stretch of coast between Port Isaac and Tintagel is bleak, inaccessible, little developed and rife with centuries of calamitous shipwrecks. 'From Padstow Point to Hartland Light / Is a watery grave by day or night.'

Though the professional wrecking along this coast may have stopped and 'Cruel Coppinger' with his smuggling lugger, the *Black Prince*, ceased to terrorise these waters, still the sea continues to reap its tragic toll. It can run mountains high and sometimes the lifeboat at Port Isaac cannot leave the harbour. In 1995 when the *Maria Asumpta*, the last old square-rigger in existence, was sailing on a westerly wind off the Rumps she was tragically smashed to pieces on the rocks and three of her crew were drowned.

To reach the wilds of Tregardock you must come first to the middle of the parish where the long, grim-looking village of Delabole hugs the road – it was once three separate hamlets called Rockhead, Medrose and Pengelly, each with its own Methodist chapel. John Wesley's influence in Cornwall was enormous. Delabole was named after the famous slate quarry which has been worked for well over four centuries and has produced a gigantic crater, four hundred feet deep. It is an astonishing sight.

Huge slabs of dark blue-grey Delabole slate is used to bound gardens and fields in and around the village and the memorials in the graveyard of the Victorian church of St John the Evangelist go black in the rain. Down the narrow lane towards the tiny chapel hamlet of Treligga, tucked up above the cliffs, the oaks are stunted and dwarfed by the wind. There are slate rubble walls, lush ferns and thorn bushes thick with sloes.

Most Cornish lanes feel haunted but perhaps this is because I read the hymn-writer S Baring-Gould's *In the Roar of the Sea* as a teenager, followed by Daphne du Maurier's *Jamaica Inn*. A bumpy track leads off to Tregardon Farm and the lane dips steeply down to reveal a view of distant Tintagel and King Arthur's castle. Treligga lies below around a bend, its whitewashed cottages and farms huddled together around the chapel, long ago converted

Left: Tregardock Cliffs, curving round towards Port Isaac

into a holiday home with rubber tree plants in its windows and a Volvo at its west door.

The track to Tregardock sinks down between brown sunburnt banks and ends at a large group of ivy-clad farm buildings hovering above the sea. Glistening granite posts support slate-roofed cattle sheds. Around the gateway to the seaward path there is silver weed growing and on the gable end of a barn, a faded and faintly alarming notice reads:

'THERE IS NO LIFEGUARD COVER AT TREGARDOCK CLIFFS. BATHING IS PROHIBITED WHEN THE TIDE IS IN.'

The path is wet and slatey, woody nightshade grows below the sloe bushes and once through the kissing gate made of huge six-foot-high bits of Delabole slate, it widens out between gorse bushes. Above the cleft, scattered with wild honeysuckle, the southward coast line comes into view, curving gently past Jacket's and Tresunger's Points to the fishing village of Port Isaac and on past Kellan Point and the ghost village of Port Quin to the furthest visible point of the islanded Rumps and the Mouls.

Steep concrete steps lead down the last dizzy height. The long sandy beach, strewn with shining black rocks and blue lagoons where cowries live, is only revealed at low tide and behind, the grim cliffs of Tregardock loom. It is a frightening place.

Tring, Hertfordshire

Tring Zoological Museum is well-loved, well cared for, completely unexpected and, on weekdays, practically empty. There is a museum cat who wanders across the varnished wooden floors, the only live animal among tens of thousands of stuffed and preserved mammals, birds, fish and insects. The ghost of the museum's creator, Walter Rothschild, is everywhere – down the corridors, on the stairs, in the study where he worked among the mahogany shelves, sitting at his huge desk and looking out through the window to the gently rising park.

Walter began collecting insects when he was seven, and continued collecting for the rest of his life. As a student he arrived at Magdalene College, Cambridge, with several dozen live kiwis. At home his specimens were already spilling out into rented rooms and sheds all over Tring. In 1899, when Walter was twenty-one, his exasperated father, the distinguished banker and first Baron Rothschild – who had already been stampeded by a herd of cassowaries in the park at Tring – gave Walter some land on the edge of the park. Here he built two small cottages (one for his books and his insect collection, and the other for a caretaker) together with a huge barn-like structure in which to house his collection of mounted specimens. This was the beginning of the museum and it

was first opened to the public in 1892. He was under no obligation to display his collections, but devoted much care and attention to the public galleries, selecting only the finest specimens for display. Over the next forty-five years the collection grew apace, as did the buildings to house it.

Up Akeman Street, away from the heart of the small town, stands the original core of the museum on the corner of what is now Park Street. It is heavily, elaborately and lavishly Rothschildian with its tile-hanging, half-timbered gables and leaded lights. Across the way is a row of mock-Tudor Rothschild almshouses, built in 1893, kempt and beautifully maintained with a small hill of stone gnomes, squirrels and assorted animals at one end of the lawn.

The lady at the museum entrance till called me 'Marm'. I was the only person in that afternoon, but I didn't feel alone because of the calm presence of the stuffed animals. The thing that struck me was how contented they all looked in their glass cases, arranged as though they were lounging about in perfect harmony. What with the mahogany fittings, there is a safe and solid atmosphere, rather like a London club in St James's.

Downstairs there are birds of paradise, silver foxes, raccoons, hyenas, lions, tigers, owls and monkeys and hundreds more. Above the black and gold ironwork supporting the encircling gallery are dozens of wooden showcases fixed to the banister rail and pitched like lecterns. You open the doors (with those satisfactory gold handles one sees on ships' furniture) to reveal thousands of bugs, beetles, grasshoppers, moths, butterflies and spiders pinned in perfect rows. The whip-scorpions are the nastiest things of all.

In a yellow room on the way to the next great barn is the most remarkable collection of zebras, one with a foal at its foot. (Walter was famous for having a carriage driven by zebras.) There are lechwes lying on the gravel in the next gallery which look positively alive, and the dimmest animal of all in the whole museum is a tiny ratty-looking animal called the Lesser Streaked Tenrec. The collection of domestic dogs is almost the best thing in the museum and includes Mick the Miller, the most legendary greyhound of the twentieth century.

The later buildings which have grown out from the museum house a major centre for bird research, where over a million skins, a million eggs and thousands of skeletons of birds preserved in alcohol lie in perfect order.

Far right: the original Tring Museum with the Dutch-gabled barn structure behind

The Valley of Rocks, **Exmoor, Devon**

The western edges of Exmoor are sublime. Vast, windswept expanses of moorland dotted with barrows, ancient earthworks and stone circles give way to soft winding combes of hanging oak woods. Shallow, brown-watered rivers with bouldered bottoms wind in the shade of sycamores and moss smothers the stone walls and the roots of beech trees. Then, from high above the Bristol Channel, the mountainous hills fall, wooded and steep, towards the shining sea.

Just west of Lynton and Lynmouth is the 'Valley of Rocks', a broad majestic sweep of extraordinary lunar landscape, scooped out during the last Ice Age above overhanging cliffs, leaving jagged pinnacles of eroded limestone like 'Ragged Jack' and 'Castle Rock'. Caves and clefts pierce the sheer rocks below. 'Was it the work of our giants, of the race of Albion?' asked the poet Robert Southey when he first came upon the Valley of Rocks at the end of the eighteenth century, the very peak of the Age of Romance. 'On the summit of the highest point of the hill, two large stones inclined against each other form a portal. Here I laid myself at length – a level platform of turf spread before me about two yards long, and then the eye fell immediately on the sea – a giddy depth. After closing my eyes a minute, it was deeply impressive to open them upon the magnificent dreariness, and the precipice and the sea.'

Nothing has changed. To reach the portal there is a pathway cut into the rock, from where you can look down on to windhovers circling below you on rising spirals of air. Across the valley, burns tumble down beside zigzagging paths where the mountain goats seem to defy gravity. In the past they were heavily culled because they used to butt the sheep over the edge of the cliffs. Today they rule the roost again and make nothing of the seemingly sheer rock faces.

In 1797 Coleridge, depressed and unwell, walked across Exmoor from Nether Stowey to stay in a farmhouse near remote St Culbone's, the smallest parish church in Britain – twelve feet, four inches wide and just over thirty feet long. Shelley drew attention to the area still further when a few years later he sped here with his sixteen-year-old bride, his first wife Harriet Westbrook, in order to escape the wrath of her parents. For nine weeks they rented a cottage in Lynmouth, tucked into a deep-gorged valley at the mouth of the East and West Lyn rivers.

But it was Richard Doddridge Blackmore (1825–1900) who brought the area to life in his romantic novel, *Lorna Doone*. Based on a band of murdering outlaws who were said to inhabit the moor near Badgery Water and from there raid farms and villages, the story of the Doones is set in the days of the Monmouth Rebellion. Lorna is portrayed as a beautiful and tragic woman who falls in love with John Ridd, a yeoman farmer from the local village of Oare. Blackmore's character Mother Meldrum is based on a real woman who lived here and 'kept her winter in this vale of rocks, sheltering from the wind and rain within the Devil's cheesering: which added greatly to her fame because all else for miles around were afraid to go near it after dark, or on a gloomy day. Under the eaves of lichened rock she had a winding passage, which none that ever I knew durst enter but herself.'

Contrasting with the sense of foreboding created by the area, there is now a cheerful cricket pitch on a plateau at the head of the valley, it being the nearest level place to Lynton and Lynmouth. The gulls seem to be the only spectators on most summer Sundays.

Right: an approaching storm at sunset, Valley of Rocks

Right: the lavishly decorated dome inside the Watts Cemetery Chapel
Inset: the Watts Gallery from outside

190

The Watts Gallery and Cemetery Chapel, Compton, Surrey

Tucked under the high chalk ridge of the Hog's Back, on the outskirts of the village of Compton, the Watts Gallery is a place of wonder. It is a homage to the painter, sculptor and visionary G F Watts, whose famous painting of Hope has inspired many, including Barack Obama, and whose statue Physical Energy still stirs the soul in Hyde Park.

Watts's talent was first nurtured by Lady Holland, but in 1851 he became the permanent guest of Mr and Mrs Thoby Prinsep. 'He came to stay for three days and stayed thirty years,' boasted his hostess, who eventually persuaded Watts to marry the actress Ellen Terry when he was forty-six and she sixteen. It was a disastrous idea and they soon parted. When he was sixty-nine he married Mary Fraser-Tytler, thirty years his junior, a Scottish designer and potter. Mindful of his health (Watts had a frail constitution and was often ill and depressed), she persuaded him to move to Compton and together they built a cottage on Down Lane designed by Ernest George.

The gallery opposite was built in 1903, a mixture of Surrey cottage style and Scottish Art Nouveau, of red-tiled gables, pebbledash, wafer-thin brick, sunburst keystones and green-glazed pottery. A fig tree grows in a little sunken garden of box hedges, rosemary and Compton Ware pots. Over the door to the lower galleries is embossed Watts's motto, 'The Utmost for the Highest'. First planned as a public gallery and as a place for Mary and her potters to work, it now houses nearly three hundred of Watts's paintings, including his self-portrait painted at the age of seventeen and *The Wounded Heron*, which was exhibited at the Royal Academy three years later. Towering over all are the original plaster models for Physical Energy and Watts's statue of Tennyson, the bronze of which stands by Lincoln Cathedral – a glorious twelve-foot-high likeness of the gloomy-looking Lincolnshire poet with his huge wolfhound. Watts died in 1904, having twice been offered a baronetcy by Gladstone which he twice refused.

During his last years, Mary proceeded to build a startling memorial to her husband – a cornucopia of Arts and Crafts. The Watts Cemetery Chapel was designed and built between 1895 and 1898, and the interior designs were completed by 1904, just before Watts's death. It stands on a little hill, a Byzantine-looking basilica of bright red brick, among cherry blossom and dark fingers of black Irish yew looking for all the world like cypresses – a recreation of Tuscany in the middle of the Home Counties. A steep path lined with flowers zigzags up towards it. Mary designed the whole thing with no professional assistance beyond that of the local builder and blacksmith, and a team of villagers trained in the pottery she had founded. 'I always hoped it would tone down,' she said, but it never did. The chapel is built on a circular and cruciform plan, part of Mary's carefully calculated symbolism – the circle of eternity with the cross of faith running through it. You walk in the Norman-arched doorway covered with terracotta heads of angels, each worked by villagers, some looking downwards in sympathy, some upward in hope. Inside is the richest, rarest display of Art Nouveau you have ever seen. A glistening green, scarlet, gold and silver mass of seraphs, angels and trees of life, their roots and tendrils winding wildly this way and that, smother the high, domed interior. Mary Watts called it her 'glorified wallpaper'. The whole surface is in fact moulded and incised in gesso, which is a sort of cross between papier-mâché and plastic. Up behind the chapel is a long cloister facing out across the valley, together with G F Watts's grave.

Wenlock Edge, Shropshire

Shropshire is the sixteenth largest county in England but the thirty-sixth in its number of inhabitants. In some places, where the strangely shaped hill formations such as the Wrekin, the Long Mynd, Clee Hill and Clun Hill jut into the sky, it feels empty, remote and reassuring. Wenlock Edge is one of the strangest hills of all. Formed of Silurian limestone and rich in fossil fauna, it looks like a saluki dog lying on a carpet of farmland; nearly three hundred feet high, eighteen miles long and never more than a mile wide. In 1809 William Gilpin described it as 'a lofty bank'. 'We saw it at a distance running like a long, black ridge, covered with wood, athwart the country... When we had attained the summit, we had no descent on the other side; this long ridge being the slope only of those grand, natural terraces, by which one tract of country sometimes descends into another.'

Much Wenlock lies below the Edge's north-eastern tip: a pleasant town of pale grey stone, half-timbering and brick, whose quiet calm owes much to the ruined Wenlock Priory, with its delicate zigzagged interlacing arches on the wall of the chapter house. The ruins are set among topiary and tall trees, next to the tantalisingly private Prior's House, and look out onto park-like surroundings where Hereford cattle graze. The country comes right up to the old town's edges. There is a half-timbered guildhall, handsome Georgian houses on Church Row, and a fashionable priest's vestment shop displaying showy brocade copes in its window near the Norman and Perpendicular church, with its over-tidy churchyard.

A track leads out towards Wenlock Edge and begins its climb past Lea Quarry and Stokes Barn and into the threatening cloud hanging over the wooded scarp. A hundred years ago A E Housman had seen the storm itself.

On Wenlock Edge the wood's in trouble:
His forest fleece the Wrekin heaves:
The gale, it plies the saplings double,
And thick on Severn snow the leaves.

At one point the track descends gently onto the line of the disused railway, which used to run from Wenlock to Church Stretton but was closed in 1951. It must have been the most spectacular train journey, hovering halfway up the precipitously hanging woods.

Above Blakeway Causeway the dark cloud lifts and to the east reveals brick farmhouses and barns studding the huge patchwork of well-hedged fields below. Oddly-shaped hills rise steeply from the farmland – the Lawley, the Wilderness and Caer Caradoc Hill – and in the distance the outline of the Long Mynd soars in great ancient folds. From up on these heights of Wenlock Edge, when the way leads briefly out of the dark woods and into the light, the views are breathtaking. Endless sweeps of Shropshire and the Welsh Marches end in the horizons of Housman's 'blue remembered hills'. To the west Corve Dale carves its beautiful river valley with wooded inlets along the Edge's lower slopes.

Through fields of sheep and under huge oak trees, I diverted to the tall shadowy Elizabethan manor of Wilderhope which looms grandly from Hope Dale, quite the gauntest and most haunted-looking house in Shropshire. During the Civil War its owner, Thomas Smallman, a major in the Royalist army, was carrying dispatches from Bridgnorth to Shrewsbury when he was captured by Cromwell's troops. They took him back to Wilderhope and locked him in an upstairs room. He escaped and galloped off but his captors followed. Along Wenlock Edge they began to catch up with him and in order to escape, the major turned off the track, kicked his horse hard and leapt off the Edge into the darkness. His fall was broken by a crab-apple tree, which he clung on to, but his horse fell and was killed. To this day, the spot is known as the 'Major's Leap'.

Left: a view of the Wrekin and the Cheshire Vale from Wenlock Edge

Wensleydale, **Yorkshire**

If you come over Middleham High Moor, even if there's a soft warm mizzle, you can still just discern the wonderful wide sweep of Wensleydale spreading out into verdant pastureland below. Myriad tree-lined walls and hedges crisscross the valley, which is speckled with silver-stoned steadings and little copses of sycamores, walnut and evergreen oaks. On the opposite slopes, great dark wedges of estate woods hang between the scars and below the heights of Redmire Moor. Rollins Lane – edged with vetches, moon daisies, St John's wort, knapweed, self-heal and greater bedstraw – leads down to Wensley, once a town but now no more than a village on the opposite banks of the River Ure. The beautiful triple-aisled church is stuffed with monuments to the legendary Scrope family, whose proud history hovers all over the dale. For centuries they were one of the most powerful families in the north of England. Brave as lions, they appeared at the forefront of every famous northern battle – Sir Henry Scrope fought at the Battle of Flodden in 1513 with a company of Wensleydale archers, together with his much-loved mastiff dog who wore a suit of armour. The name was lost when Mary Scrope married Charles Paulet, a supporter and friend of William of Orange, who made him the first Duke of Bolton. A man of infinite whim, he would not open his mouth for days at a time in case some evil spirit should get in. He refused to go out in daylight, had amazing bacchanalian orgies in a banqueting hall in the woods and hunted his hounds at night by torchlight. It was he who decided to abandon the old Bolton Castle, which had been pretty bashed up by the Parliamentarians anyway, and build the grand new Bolton Hall in the late 1670s.

The Scropes were relative newcomers to this pocket of Arcadia – on and below the moors there are two Roman camps, a Roman villa and a Stone Age sauna bath, and the moors are pockmarked with residues of Roman open-cast mining for lead and silver. Along Leyburn Shawl, in the depths of Warren Wood, a secret cavern covered with Neolithic paintings was discovered in the 1830s and has since been lost again in deep undergrowth. In some places you can find seven different orchids within twenty minutes of walking – green-winged, burnt tip, fragrant, spotted, bee, early purple and pyramid. This wildly romantic slice of Wensleydale is still well cared for and well loved by the present Bolton family who have planted nearly 30,000 broad-leaved indigenous trees and taken over the day-today running of the Castle, keeping it open and afloat against all odds.

If you take the back lane from Wensley towards Bolton Castle, a footpath leads down past the gaunt and majestic rebuild of Bolton Hall (reduced to a shell by fire in 1902), past its forgotten terraced lawns and lost water garden, sprinkled with sycamore saplings, rosebay willow herb and ferns, past old stud buildings, vestiges of a glorious racing past when the Boltons bred Jack Spigot, the winner of the St Leger in 1821, and on through gentle parkland sloping down towards the shallow, brown-watered River Ure. Here the double-arched, grandly gate-piered Lords Bridge spans its width.

Further on up the valley is the little village of Castle Bolton, a straight street of cottages with small, walled front gardens which give on to wide grass verges. At the end stands the dream castle – perfectly symmetrical. Square towers rise from each corner, joined by walls which enclose the internal courtyard. It was built in the fourteenth century as much for elegance as for defence. Here Mary Queen of Scots was held captive for six months with her retinue of twenty-five staff, and from these high windows the view is ever the same, unfurling southwards across the dale to the great heights of Penhill Crags.

Left: Bolton Castle

Whitby, **Yorkshire**

Yorkshire people are so friendly. You feel it sitting in the cosy bustle of Elizabeth Botham and Sons' tea rooms (established 1865) on Whitby's West Side. Towered plates of Yorkshire curd tarts, ginger cakes and their famous lemon buns are delivered with beaming smiles to your table. I said to my waitress, 'This is as good as Betty's in Harrogate.' 'Madam,' she replied. 'It's better.'

Between high hills, the town is set in a dramatically deep cleft where the River Esk widens towards the sea, secreting an upper harbour full of boats and clinking masts in the town's midst and ending its twenty-mile journey in the Lower Harbour. Two lighthouses stand sentinel on the claw-shaped breakwaters to guide ships in between the treacherous cliffs. On Fish Quay there is a bandstand, a fish market and the white stucco Magpie Café which Rick Stein says serves the best fish and chips in the world.

Whitby's West Side is the younger side of town. A statue of Captain Cook commands the cliff top, looking out across the harbour where his ships *Endeavour*, *Resolution* and *Adventure* were built and from where he sailed around the world. There is an arch made of a whale's jaw bone boasting the town's history as a whaling port, which reached its peak in the eighteenth century. The industry's most famous captain was William Scoresby, who landed 533 whales in his career and invented the 'crow's nest'.

Whitby's street lamps used to be lit by a gas made from whale oil. West Cliff, with Whitby Sands below, developed apace through the nineteenth century with elegant terraces, a stunning Victorian church and streets of red-brick villas with holly trees in their gardens around Fishburn Park and Pannett Park. In the latter, the Whitby Museum boasts an amazing collection of wild birds and fossils including pieces of Whitby jet. There are Cook and Scoresby mementoes and also the gruesome severed hand of a murderer, which was used by local burglars as a charm to send their victims into a deep sleep.

Gothic to the hilt, Whitby's famous visitor, Bram Stoker, described the town in *Dracula*, elaborating on the real wrecking of a Russian ship when only a dog survived and somehow scrambled ashore. Stoker made the dog head straight for St Mary's graveyard, as dramatic as any in the country, on the treacherous wind-blown eastern cliff top. Connected to the west side across a swing bridge, the old town huddles below the cliff. The cobbled Church Street leads slowly up the hill, past the old market house with its bulging Tuscan columns, past the Whitby rowing club, past ginnels sloping riverwards giving glimpses across the low-tide mud to Fish Quay and to backyards full of washing, past shops selling crabs and navy-blue jerseys called 'ganseys', and on up the 199-step climb to St Mary's Church, 'the Sailor's Church'.

The view of Whitby from this high bluff is terrific, and so is the inside of the squat and ancient church, chock-a-block with monuments, beautiful box pews, a three-decker pulpit, galleries and stairs made by ship builders – a moving testament to a sailors' community to which the graveyard further testifies. Beyond the church, Whitby Abbey's gaunt remains rise on the site of St Hilda's seventh-century foundations. This is perhaps the most spectacular and venerable holy site in the Kingdom, where the synod of Whitby committed the English church to the Roman rather than the Celtic rite. After the Dissolution, the Cholmley family built a house beside the Abbey which became a roofless shell after interminable storms (it now houses a museum). Its hauntingly beautiful Renaissance facade looks out to sea.

Right: looking inland up the River Esk
Inset: the Magpie Café, famous for its fish and chips

White Horse Hill, Oxfordshire

Before the gods that made the gods
Had seen their sunrise pass,
The White Horse of the White Horse Vale
Was cut out of the grass.

G K Chesterton

All is well with the world up here on the top of the downs, where the affinity with the sky is strong and there is always a speck of a lark and somewhere the call of a peewit. On the steep slopes, where chemical sprays do not drift, there are bee orchids, patches of bright blue squill, harebells, early purple orchids, nettle-leaved bellflower, rock-rose, lady's bedstraw, hawk's beard, agrimony, mignonette, scabious and knapweed. The White Horse, with its spindly legs outstretched at full gallop, is incised in chalk like a modern painting across the soft, steep slope of downland. It was designed to be seen from afar or perhaps from the air and can only be recognised as a horse from a mile or so distant. The Manger runs in a wide curving sweep down and away from the White Horse in a series of undulating billows, and moved Aldous Huxley's hero in *Crome Yellow* to be 'deeply overcome by the beauty of those deeply embayed combes, scooped in the flanks of the ridge beneath him... they were as fine as the lines on a human body, they were informed with the subtlety of art'. Directly below the White Horse is a strange flat-topped pudding-shaped hill where St George is said to have killed the dragon and which looks as though it has been sculpted.

Various archaeological digs have come to no definitive conclusions as to the origin or purpose of the White Horse, and long may it remain a mystery. The moving thing about it is that it is still there and has captured man's imagination for well over three thousand years. Whatever belief system has been in place the horse has been maintained and the chalk scoured. (It would soon grass over if left to nature.) The sense of continuity is consoling.

'And then what a hill is White Horse Hill!' wrote Thomas Hughes, author of *Tom Brown's Schooldays*, who was born in Uffington in the vale below. 'There it stands straight up above all the rest, nine hundred feet above the sea, and the boldest, bravest shape for a chalk hill that you ever saw ... The ground falls rapidly on all sides. Was there ever such turf in the whole world? You sink up to your ankles at every step, and yet the spring of it is delicious ... It is a place you won't ever forget – a place to open a man's soul and make him prophesy as he looks down on that great vale spread as the garden of the Lord before him and wave on wave of the mysterious downs behind: and to the right and left, the chalk hills running away into the distance, along which he can trace the old Roman [*sic*] road, "the Ridgeway" ("the rudge" as the country folk call it), keeping straight along the highest back of the hills.'

The Ridgeway, the oldest track in Europe, runs like a white ribbon, lonely and exposed, stretching away for miles behind the castle. Prehistory unfurls beside it: the vestiges of Stone Age farming, mysterious barrows or long barrows, like Wayland's Smithy, encircled in towering wind-blown beech, strip lynchets carved into combes, Iron-Age hill forts, standing stones, dewponds in ash tree-filled dells and off in a hidden valley the deserted village of Snap where, in midwinter, the ruined cottage walls are visible in the leafless tangle of trees and undergrowth: a haunting and melancholy place.

The feeling that man has travelled the Ridgeway for over ten thousand years is always there: 'I do not believe anything of the past ever quite disappears.' A habitual Ridgeway walker, Kenneth Grahame, who lived nearby, wrote of it, '...such a track is in some sort humanly companionable; it seems to almost lead you by the hand.' However empty and desolate the surrounding landscape may look on a bleak day, you never feel completely alone here.

Far left: the view from the White Horse towards Dragon Hill and the Manger
Inset: White Horse Hill, illustration by Arthur Hughes (1832–1915) from *Tom Brown's School Days* by Thomas Hughes

Whitehaven, **Cumbria**

Whitehaven is out on a limb: remote and unvisited. Coming to it from Cleaton Moor, where the great mountains of Copeland Forest rise gigantic and snow-capped to the east, the glistening Solway Firth widens out into the Irish Sea ahead. Southwards the Cumbrian coast stretches down to Barrow-in-Furness, and Scotland looms on the far side of the Firth to the north. Whitehaven is a tremendous place. It was always an industrial town and the North country strength is everywhere. Seeing the town for the first time in its deep basin scooped out between the cliffs is awe-inspiring.

The Cumbrian landscape artist Matthias Read's masterpiece, *A Bird's Eye View of Whitehaven*, painted in the 1730s, shows the town's ordered formality with its grid pattern of streets running back from the ship-filled harbour. Today, curling down the hill into what must be one of the best and most undiscovered Georgian towns in the country, much of the original layout is still in evidence: tall handsome colour-washed houses with contrasting window-surrounds line the dead-straight streets and sometimes end with a perfect, dead-on view of a church. Overlooking the harbour, the box-like church of St James's, with its extravagant interior, is one of the most beautiful Georgian churches in the north of England. All is testament to Whitehaven's glory days when, after Bristol, it was the biggest port in Britain, competing with Newcastle and Liverpool. A modern statue down on the quay tells of the mining industry which was the key to Whitehaven's success. It was a company town through and through, built by one family on one industry.

Until the seventeenth century, Whitehaven was a small fishing village, an adjunct to the religious settlement of St Bees. It was the Lowther family who were to change its fortunes when Sir Christopher Lowther bought the village lock, stock and barrel, as well as the surrounding estate. He laid out plans for the development of coal mines and set about creating a port from which to export the coal to Ireland. A shipbuilding industry sprang up and iron ore was mined locally to supplement the coal exports. Whitehaven grew in stature, and Lowther's son John, inspired by Sir Christopher Wren's restoration of London and backed by an enormous bank balance, began to build one of the first planned towns in England.

By 1685 Whitehaven had a population of a thousand, and twenty-five years later it had trebled. Trade with the Caribbean and America blossomed and Whitehaven became a major importer of rum, sugar and tobacco, vying with London. To the designs of the most fashionable architect of the day, Robert Adam, John Lowther built himself a grandiose castellated mansion known as 'the Castle' which overlooked the town from its hill-side site. By the late eighteenth century Whitehaven was a large and important town with a total of 448 ships.

Whitehaven had reached its peak. The American War of Independence put paid to its chief import trade and the town began its gradual decline. Its overland remoteness worked against it, as did the finite size of its harbour which could no longer accommodate the ever-increasing size of ships. By the twentieth century the town suffered further through the decline of the mining industry. The large chemical factory, which sprang up in the 1940s and gave the town such hope, closed in 2007.

Whitehaven is fighting back. Its glorious Georgian past is being made much of: the visitors to the Mining Museum are steadily increasing, the marina is attracting pleasure boats by the dozen, the Castle has been turned into private apartments, and the Whitehaven Male Voice Choir sings to large crowds which pack the generous nave and encircling upper galleries of St James's Church.

Left: winter view of Whitehaven looking over the south harbour

Widecombe-in-the-Moor, Devon

Winter is the time to go, 'all along, down along, Widecombe way'. The tourist buses no longer crawl towards this perfect English village. The place is quiet. The deep, dark lanes which wind to Widecombe from Northway and Dunstone, from Natsworthy, Cockingford and Blackaton, are empty.

I came to Widecombe in the early morning over the moor from Bonehill Down. It was a sublime day, horizon after horizon rose above wisps of mist, as in a Caspar David Friedrich painting. The valley of the River Webburn fell away into a dark crevice of alders and willows and there, on the opposite bank, the village stood against its patchwork backdrop of high-hedged fields, topped by granite-strewn moor. All around lie the remains of roundhouses, cairns, hut circles, barrows and old tin mines – evidence that this area has been inhabited for three or four thousand years.

The church, known as the 'Cathedral of the Moor' because of its one hundred and twenty-foot-high tower, provides a beacon for miles around. However familiar this picture of perfect England, however overused on calendars and Christmas cards, it is still extraordinary. The church of St Pancras, built with tinners' money, dwarfs all around it and in the past would have been packed with miners and members of the farming community who lived in outlying longhouses in this enormous parish, nearly seven miles by five. The church stands on the site of a thirteenth-century building which was rebuilt and enlarged in the early 1600s in the Perpendicular style. Huddled round the tiny village square are the Church House, an early sixteenth-century granite structure with a portico (once serving as an almshouse and school), the Glebe House and The Old Inn – all sparkling granite and looking as though they have grown from the landscape.

On the afternoon of 21st October 1638 the vicar, George Lyde, was conducting a service here when a terrible storm broke out. The north-east pinnacle of the church tower was struck by lightning and fell through the roof and, according to the church wardens at the time, Peter and Sylvester Mann, who recorded the tragedy in every detail, a great fiery ball passed right through the church injuring a number of people. Four were killed on the spot and others died later from their injuries. Money melted in peoples' purses but the purses remained intact. The landlady of the inn at Poundsgate, four miles away, testified that on that Sunday afternoon a horseman on his way to Widecombe called for a drink and she noticed that as the ale passed down his throat it sizzled, like water being poured on hot iron. Superstition ascribes the storm to a visitation of Satan. Richard Hill, the village schoolmaster, wrote some quaint commemorative verses about the disaster which are painted on boards in the tower.

But it was the Reverend Sabine Baring-Gould, vicar of a neighbouring parish and author of 'Onward Christian Soldiers', who was responsible for making Widecombe so famous. He was touring in the area and heard an old lady singing to herself as she worked. He followed her around with pen and paper in hand (she wouldn't stay still long enough to sing the whole song) and recorded one of the most famous folk songs in history: 'Tom Pearce, Tom Pearce, lend me your grey mare / All along, down along, out along, lee / For I want to go down to Widecombe Fair...' The fair still takes place, although the local white-faced Dartmoor sheep, known as 'Widecombes', which used to be bought and sold, are no longer in evidence. The fair is kept going by a few committed locals dedicated to its survival. Dartmoor ponies are shown and there are local produce stalls, races, tugs of war and sheepdog trials.

Right: Widecombe-in-the-Moor in Dartmoor National Park

Wilton's Music Hall, **London**

Hidden down an alley at the back of Cable Street, in the midst of Tower Hamlets' 1960s redevelopment, is a row of five modest Georgian houses. Converted by Matthew Eltham in the late 1820s to become The Prince of Denmark public house, they tell nothing of what lies behind them. Peeling double doors set between decorated plasterwork panels of fruit and flowers lead into the old pub, a higgledy-piggledy hotchpotch of different rooms at varying levels. But beyond the central paved lobby and the wide stairway is one of the East End's hidden wonders – Wilton's Music Hall. This astonishing and magical space fills the site at the back of the building and is completely landlocked by the surrounding properties. The ghosts of the old performers still haunt the stage and it isn't hard to imagine the raked floor and balconies crammed with gaiety and noise. Its atmosphere is moving. It is, after all, London's last music hall, left just as it always was .

The first music hall in England was built onto the Canterbury Tavern in Lambeth in 1852 by Charles Morton. It was an overnight success and inspired the birth of music halls throughout the country – by 1875 there were 375 in greater London alone. John

Right: the auditorium
Inset: Wilton's entrance on Graces Alley

Wilton, who had bought The Prince of Denmark by then – the first pub in London to boast mahogany counters and fittings – was hot on Morton's heels and built his music hall in 1853. When he acquired the adjoining properties and their gardens he replaced them with a vastly enlarged 'grand music hall' designed by Jacob Maggs, which opened in 1859. Maggs created a big rectangular room with an apse at the back and a high stage. The vaulted ceiling has ornamental fretted ribs from which, in Wilton's heyday, hung a 'sun-burner' chandelier of three hundred gas jets and 27,000 cut crystals which illuminated the mirrored hall. A single balcony runs round three sides, supported by 'barley sugar' columns made of cast iron.

Wilton's was a sensation. It hosted one of the first British performances of the can-can, and the legendary Arthur Lloyd – Scottish baritone, comedian and favourite with royalty – performed there on many occasions. Perhaps Wilton's most popular performer was George Leybourne, who achieved film-star status with the song he wrote and sang, 'Champagne Charlie'. The song became such a hit that his wages rose from £25 to £125 a week. On top of that he received sponsorship money from Moët & Chandon because he was advertising their product. Leybourne sported a top hat and elaborate whiskers, rode around London with his own carriage and four, and was seldom without a beautiful woman on his arm.

Not only is the theatre in its present surroundings so utterly unexpected, its survival story is extraordinary. Since its glamorous beginnings as one of England's first music halls, when the birth of cabaret and public entertainment for the masses was on the wing, Wilton's has continued to play a significant role in the East End's history. In 1889 during the first-ever dockers' strike two thousand meals a day were provided for them by a Methodist mission who had recently acquired the buildings. It also acted as the headquarters for East Enders who gathered to stop Oswald Mosley in the Cable Street Riots of 1936 and as a shelter for bombed-out families in the Second World War. By the 1950s it had become a rag-sorting depot.

This forgotten, neglected and secret place miraculously survived demolition during the postwar slum clearances in the 1960s because of a campaign to get it listed spearheaded by my father, John Betjeman. It was subsequently bought by the Greater London Council and is now leased to the Wilton's Music Hall Trust.

Winterborne Came, **Dorset**

Just south of Dorchester, below the sweep of Came Down and not far from the lost village of Winterborne Farringdon, William Barnes, the Dorset poet and philologist, is buried in the churchyard of St Peter's Church. He was rector here in this tiny hamlet of Winterborne Came from 1862 until his death in 1886. Although the thatched Regency rectory in which Barnes lived is on the now-busy main road to Weymouth, the church itself is hidden a quarter of a mile away in a secret backwater. A lane runs along a valley beside the Upper Winterborne River and then turns towards St Peter's, which stands in the shadow of a great walled garden and trees. It is a simple and unassuming church with a barrel-vaulted ceiling, double-table tomb effigies and some sixteenth-century hatchments. The churchyard runs into the park of the beautiful Palladian Came House, which is built of the palest silvery limestone which turns almost white in the sunlight. The stone was quarried just over the downs at Portland and is arguably the most beautiful building stone in England. (Christopher Wren demanded only this stone and it was used to build St Paul's Cathedral.)

Came House was designed by the Dorset architect Francis Cartwright and was his proudest achievement. On his monument in Blandford St Mary Church are carved a T-square, dividers and a scroll in which is incised an elevation of Came House.

For me the romance of the place is to do with William Barnes, whose lyrical poetry written in Dorset dialect was so much admired by his friends Alfred Tennyson, Gerard Manley Hopkins and, above all, by his close neighbour Thomas Hardy. A farmer's son, Barnes first worked as a solicitor's clerk and then as a school-master before being ordained into the church. He married Julia Miles in 1827 and was devastated by her death over thirty years later. Many of his poems describe his love for her. His writing displays great tenderness, love of his surroundings and of the humble country way of life. His poem 'My Orcha'd in Linden Lea' was set to music by Vaughan Williams.

Barnes was passionately interested in language and was fluent in Greek, Latin and several European languages. He campaigned for the purification of English by the removal of Greek, Latin and other foreign influences so that it might be better understood by those without classical education. The word 'photograph', for instance, which is derived from the Greek for 'light' and 'writing', he suggested should become 'sun-print' instead. He liked the words 'worlore' for botany, 'pushwainling' for perambulator and 'nipperlings' for forceps.

Hardy and his friend Mr Edmund Gosse visited Barnes on his deathbed, having walked from Hardy's house on the outskirts of Dorchester. 'It is curious that he is dying as picturesquely as he lived,' wrote Mr Gosse. 'We found him in bed in his study, his face turned to the window, where the sun came streaming in through flowering plants ... He had a scarlet bed gown on, a kind of soft biretta of dark red wool on his head, from which his long white hair escaped onto the pillow, his grey beard grown very long upon his breast.'

Barnes's obituary in the *Saturday Review* read: 'There is no doubt that he is the best pastoral poet we possess, the most sincere, the most genuine, the most theocritan; and that the dialect is but a very thin veil hiding from us some of the most delicate and finished verse written in our time.'

Right: Came House and
St Peter's Church

Right: the interior of
St Andrew's Church in
Winterborne Tomson
Inset: the exterior

Winterborne Tomson, Dorset

St Andrew's is the sort of church that makes you believe in God. Its simple perfection cannot fail to move you and it is worth driving many miles to see. What remains of the tiny hamlet of Winterborne Tomson lies a stone's throw from the thundering Wimborne to Blandford road in meadowy country straddling the Winterborne – a small chalk river which, as its name implies, almost dries up in the summer and becomes no more than a whisper. Some maps don't even mark Winterborne Tomson, noting only its bigger neighbours: Winterborne Zelstone to the east, with its self-conscious cottages and wonderful ox's head gargoyle on its squat-towered church and, clinging to the river upstream, Winterbornes Kingston, Whitechurch, Clenston and Houghton.

The church stands in a working farmyard of barns, both ancient and modern, near the seventeenth-century manor-house whose north facade is more thrilling than its south. As you open the churchyard gate you can see across the flat fields and the river, beyond a line of poplars, the many gables and towering chimneys of Anderson Manor, a grand Elizabethan house of a strange plum-coloured brick with chalk-stone dressings, tantalisingly unopen to the public.

From the outside the simple Norman church of lichen-covered brownstone rubble and flint, with its small weather-boarded bell turret, resembles a river tug-boat. Its walls have sloped outwards over the centuries. The inside, with its stone-flagged floor and undulating lime-washed walls, exceeds expectation. The simple wagon roof is curved around the apse with finely carved bosses, where the oak ribs intersect. The church was beautifully renovated with oak fittings in the early eighteenth century and given the finest set of box pews, a two-decker pulpit with tester, a chancel screen, altar rails and a gallery by the benevolent William Wake, a native of Blandford who became Archbishop of Canterbury and who loved the church. The oak, bleached by the light flooding in through the clear-glassed southern windows for the last three hundred years, is of the palest watery buff-colour. The church possesses an extraordinary calm, for there is nothing that jars the eye. All is harmonious.

If this church is a monument to God then it is also a monument to the organisation that saved it from becoming a ruin. By the 1920s, St Andrew's had fallen into a sad state of decay and was 'given over to donkeys, dogs, pigs and fowl'. Albert Reginald Powys, who lived in Dorset, was the secretary of the Society for the Protection of Ancient Buildings and through its auspices determined to restore the church for posterity. The son of a Victorian vicar, an architect and writer of (among other books) *The Repair of Ancient Buildings* and *The English Parish Church*, he was one of eleven children, many of whom grew up to become distinguished in the arts. Three of his brothers – John Cowper, Theodore Francis and Llewellyn – and one of his sisters, Catherine, were all well-known writers, essayists and poets, and his sister Gertrude an accomplished artist.

Money needed to be raised for the restoration of St Andrew's and A R Powys had the idea to sell the Society's many letters from Thomas Hardy to pay for it. Hardy had been a member of the SPAB for forty-seven years, and since he had started his career as a church architect and loved Winterborne Tomson, it seemed a fitting thing to do. In the true spirit of the Society's founder, William Morris, A R Powys supervised the most sensitive and gentle restoration. A plaque in the church, cut by the gifted Dorset engraver Reynolds Stone, pays tribute to him.

St Andrew's is now cared for by the Churches Conservation Trust which looks after over three hundred and forty of England's churches which are no longer in use, but whose history, beauty and atmosphere, and whose familiar place in the landscape, make them worthy of safeguarding.

Wistman's Wood, Dartmoor, Devon

Woods get forgotten. They are places of mysterious beauty. Each wood has its own character and its own ancestry and, in the right circumstances, an awe-inspiring permanence – the Burren in Ireland has looked just the same as it does today for eight or nine thousand years, and parts of Wayland Wood in Norfolk, the supposed setting for *Babes in the Wood*, are truly primeval. But the tiny Wistman's Wood, laced with local legend, is perhaps the strangest and most mystical of all – a vestige of the offspring of prehistoric woodland.

Nowhere suits England's wild winter weather better than Dartmoor; nowhere is more relentlessly melancholy. The dark moorland will take you back thousands of years with its ragged peaks appearing through the mist, its stone circles, ancient encampments and abandoned villages. But best of all is Wistman's Wood – a silent, unadulterated and secret place. If you go to the very middle of the moor, just up from Princetown and its prison, near Two Bridges where the only two roads which cross the moor meet, there is a path which leads northwards towards Cocks Hill. From here it is a mile and a half's walk along the side of a wide, long valley of the West Dart, gradually climbing into bleaker, more desolate country.

From a distance the wood looks like a patch of low scrub, grey-brown against the moorland on the eastern slopes of the river. As you approach, its magic grows. I think there is a fear of woods embedded in our subconscious from the days when the 'wild-wood' covered the land. Today only nine per cent of the country is covered in trees and that is mostly in Scotland. Woods are tamer places now but they are still irrevocably laced into our literature and folklore. Wistman's Wood is not the sort of tall dark forest feared by Little Red Riding Hood but more the mystical stunted woodland where Shakespearean heroes lose their way in a tangle of low-hanging branches – 'this desert inaccessible / Under the shade of melancholy boughs.'

Wistman's dwarf oaks crouch in gnarled and twisted forms, clinging to and growing up between huge moss-covered blocks of moorland granite. Many of their mossy limbs rest on the leafy woodland floor. There are bilberries and brambles scattered among them and feathery ferns growing from the branches, including the filmy fern. There are red foxes and adders sunning themselves on the boulders in spring.

The Reverend Swette visited the wood at the end of the eighteenth century with great apprehension. 'It is hardly possible to conceive,' he wrote of Wistman's, 'anything of the sort so grotesque ... Silence seemed to have taken up her abode in this sequestered wood – and to a superstitious mind some impression would have occurred approaching to dread, or sacred horror.' Noel Carrington, a grocer's son from Plymouth turned poet, writes concurrently mourning the wood's slow death: 'Dishonour – old – dreary in aspect – silently decays / The Lonely Wood of Wistman.'

The Victorian romantic Eliza Bray believed that Wistman's Wood was a sacred grove of the druids and proceeded to devote a whole chapter of her book *Druids on Dartmoor* to prove her point. Others suggest that the wood is the kennels where the diabolical 'Wish Hounds' are kept, and that on dark misty nights their baying can be heard. Sometimes the ghost of a dog called 'Jumbo' is seen chasing after rabbits.

The nature writer and film-maker Roger Deakin likened the trees at Wistman's to gigantic spiders. For me it is the 'dark but gentle ambush' described by Louis MacNeice in his poem 'Woods':

And always we walk out again. The patch
Of sky at the end of the path grows...

The valley opens out towards the long slow walk down to the road and to the roaring fire in the Two Bridges Hotel.

Left: Wistman's Wood

Wooler, Northumberland

Northumberland is gigantic, archaic and a foreign country to those who live in the South. If you spend time in its rural outback, it's hard to understand a word anyone is saying: the language is far nearer to Scandinavian than it is to Anglo-Saxon, and a visit to Wooler is as good as going abroad. Although Thomas Sharp's 1952 Shell Guide refers to Wooler as 'a mostly nineteenth-century town without much character', I know different.

The small town sits comfortably on a hillside below the huge looming Cheviots, which form a dark brown backdrop halfway up the sky. Prehistoric settlements and isolated villages lie hidden up dry valleys, and on Coldmartin Hill there is a ruined peel tower beside a little loch. In its early days, when the warring between Scotland and England ebbed and flowed and the Battle of Humbleton Hill was won or lost, Wooler was nothing more than a tiny hamlet situated in an 'ill-cultivated country under the influence of vast mountains from whence it was subject to impetuous rains'. But when Robert de Muschamp was made the first Baron of Wooler by Henry I he got a charter for a market, and from then on Wooler's status as a centre of the wool industry grew. Today Wooler Livestock Market, originally started by a group of farmers in the late nineteenth century, is renowned throughout this sheep-breeding county of north Northumberland. Every Wednesday sees an average of three thousand sheep and a hundred cattle through its pens, and Wooler's bars – The Anchor Inn, The Angel Inn, The Black Bull, The Red Lion and The Tankerville Arms – are bustling.

Wooler's ordinary, modest houses are built in the local deep plum-coloured stone. There are good gardens behind, and every so often an archway opens on to a back alley – the one next to the newsagent leads to the pretty arched-windowed Presbyterian Meeting House, where over three hundred people once filled the pews on a Sunday. There is a stalwart-looking mid-Victorian Catholic church and a fine little house beside it, opposite the doctor's surgery. Further out along Burnhouse Road are two particularly fine 1920s pebble-dashed bungalows (Numbers 44 and 45).

At the other end of Wooler is St Mary's Church, the Georgian interior of which has been so zealously redecorated and is so brightly lit that it feels like a hospital operating theatre – bright white, clinical and rather nerve-wracking. Below the town, the River Glen winds picturesquely through flat meadows which provide a perfect site for the famous annual Glendale Show, where there is fierce competition between local farmers.

Some locals refer to Wooler as 'the centre of the universe', and it is as good a candidate as any. A visitor in the 1860s described the town as 'such a place as you would expect to see in the heart of a country; decidedly rustic, with roofs of thatch here and there to temper aspiring notions, with shops that remind you of the days of George III, but yet with homely prosperity. The parson preached in his thatched church until it was burned down about a hundred years ago [1763]. With two thousand inhabitants it is an important metropolis, drawing folks to its fairs and markets for miles around, and, as I saw, careful to send its boys and girls to school.'

Today the shops along the high street are as homely as ever. There is a family butcher and no breath of a chain except for a small and garish food store. The Glendale Pharmacy has glass bottles full of different coloured liquids on the top of its mahogany shelves. The unisex hairdresser is called 'Wavelengths', and the local art shop carries a good line in second-hand Fifties clothes and paste jewellery. In among endless bric-a-brac, some set out in the cold upstairs bedrooms of his high-street shop, Hamish Dunn has a fine second-hand book department, with a good local topography section and a lot of Walter Scott.

Far left: Wooler High Street from St Mary's Church. Inset: sheep at the Livestock Market

Wreay, Cumbria

Lovelorn Victorian women with wild imaginations and money to back their dreams seem to abound in the North of England. Louisa, Lady Waterford, for instance, whose dashing husband was killed in a hunting accident before he was forty, set about an exemplary social building programme at Ford in Northumberland to assuage her grief. The crowning glory among her new cottages was a fine village school whose walls are covered in religious murals which she painted over several years.

At about the same time, on the other side of the Cheviots, Sarah Losh was mourning the death not only of her only sister, Catherine, but also of her neighbour, Major William Thain. Sarah was beautiful, dignified, passionate about the arts, and had spent time in Italy. She was brought up surrounded by interesting and innovative people – her father, a friend of Wordsworth, and her uncle William, a friend of George Stephenson, had founded an ironworks in Newcastle which made them a small fortune. Sarah was well equipped to mastermind the building of the extraordinary church and mausoleum which today stand testament to her love and her faith in God.

The village green, with its central seat around a flagpole, the small straggle of cottages and the church shaded by beech and yew are easily missed. Wreay is set in the flat, undistinguished farmland of the Solway Plain just south of Carlisle, squashed in a tight sandwich between the M6 motorway and the mainline railway, but all that is forgotten when you arrive. It is worth breaking any journey on the M6 to stop off and have your heart lifted by Sarah Losh's moving masterpiece.

Sarah lived at the family home of Woodside, a long walk up a straight, treeless road from the dilapidated church of St Mary's. In 1840 she decided to rebuild the church and by 1842, after spending £1,200, it was ready to be consecrated. Fast work – but she had the advantage of being on the spot and of employing most of the villagers. Her gardener did the wood-carving, including the panel on the west door which represents a gourd being eaten by a caterpillar. The windows are bright with coloured leaves in black glass and fragments of ancient glass, brought from the ruins of the archbishop's palace in Paris by Sarah's cousin, William Losh.

The local stonemason, Mr Hindson, was sent to Italy for a few months to improve his skills and returned to enliven the plain Romanesque church with the natural world. The chancel arch is decorated with palm trees and angels, the alabaster font with pomegranates and butterflies which Sarah helped to carve, an eagle supports the lectern, a pelican the reading desk, a hollowed oak stump in stone is the pulpit. Sarah's recurring theme – the conflict between life and death, light and darkness – pervades. Angels triumph over bats and dragons, chrysalises and butterflies represent death and resurrection. But the most poignant carvings of all are the many pine cones – classical symbols of eternal life. A real pine cone had been sent to Sarah by Major Thain, the local hero who had fought at Waterloo but who was eventually killed in the Afghan War in 1842. Perhaps Sarah, or maybe Catherine, was in love with him. The mausoleum in the churchyard houses a delicately carved alabaster figure of Catherine clothed in a simple tunic, holding a pine cone in her hand.

Architectural historians are impressed but puzzled over Wreay. They worry that its building anticipated Ruskinian dogma in the use of estate labour and simple local labourers as craftsmen, and that the stylised carvings of nature look as though they belong to the Arts and Crafts Movement of the early 1900s. But Sarah Losh was simply half a century ahead of her time with her brave new style and her wild imagination. Not everything has to be put in a box. I'm glad Wreay is out on a limb.

Left: St Mary's Church, restored by Sarah Losh between 1840 and 1842

Contact information

APPLEBY HORSE FAIR
The next fair takes place on
2nd–8th June 2011.
www.applebyfair.org

ASHDOWN HOUSE
The house is tenanted and
access is limited to the staircase and roof (reached via 100
steps). Open April to October
from 2pm–5pm on Wednesdays
and Saturdays only.
Admission by guided tour to
house at 2.15, 3.15 and 4.15.
Numbers limited.
Last admission 30 minutes
before closing.
The woodland is open all year
round from dawn to dusk,
apart from Fridays.
01494 755 569
www.nationaltrust.org.uk

BEVERLEY MINSTER
01482 868 540
www.beverleyminster.org
Beverley Minster, Minster
Yard North, Beverley,
East Riding, Yorkshire
HU17 0DP

BISHOP'S PALACE, WELLS
Open daily, 13th February
to 22nd December. Opening
hours: 10.30am–6pm during
British Summer Time;
10.30am–4.30pm during the
winter. Last admission one
hour before closing.
01749 988 111
www.bishopspalacewells.co.uk
The Bishop's Palace, Wells,
Somerset BA5 2PD

ST MARY'S CHURCH,
BOTTESFORD
01949 842 859
www.stmarysbottesford.co.uk

BREAMORE HOUSE
The Elizabethan Manor House
and Countryside Museum are
open for visitors from April
until the end of September.
April: open on Tuesdays only.
May to September: open
Sundays to Thursdays, and on
Bank Holidays. Museum opens
at 1pm, Manor House at 2pm
(guided tours only).
01725 512 468
www.breamorehouse.com
Breamore House,
Nr. Fordingbridge,
Hampshire SP6 2DF

CARTMEL RACECOURSE
01539 536 340
www.cartmel-racecourse.co.uk
Cartmel Racecourse,
Cartmel Grange-over-Sands,
Cumbria LA11 6QF

CHATSWORTH HOUSE
Open every day except over
Christmas.
House from 11am–5.30pm
(last admission 4.30pm).
Garden open 11am–6pm
(last admission 5pm).
01246 565 300
www.chatsworth.org
Chatsworth, Bakewell,
Derbyshire DE45 1PP

CHETTLE HOUSE
The House and Gardens are
open on Easter Sunday, and
then on the first and second
Sundays of each month, April–
October, from 11am–5pm.
01258 830 858
www.chettlehouse.co.uk
Chettle House, Chettle
Blandford Forum DT11 8DB

CLUN
www.clun.org.uk

COMPTON WATTS
GALLERY
Closed to the public
for restoration.
Planned reopening in late 2010.
For up-to-date information,
see contact details below.
01483 810 235
www.wattsgallery.org.uk
Watts Gallery, Down Lane,
Compton, Surrey
GU3 1DQ

COTTESBROOKE HALL
Open 3rd May to
30th September 2010.
May and June: Wednesdays
and Thursdays, 2pm–5.30pm.
July, August and September:
Thursdays, 2pm–5.30pm.
01604 505 808
www.cottesbrookehall.co.uk
Cottesbrooke Hall
Northampton
NN6 8PF

CRAGSIDE
Open 13th March to 31st
October 2010, Tuesdays to
Sundays. Times vary.
See contact details below.
01669 620 333
www.nationaltrust.org.uk
Cragside, Rothbury
Morpeth, Northumberland
NE65 7PX

DORNEY COURT
Dorney Court is open to the
public in April and May,
Mondays to Fridays, and the
two Bank Holiday Sundays in
May. Closed August 2010.
01628 604 638
www.dorneycourt.co.uk
Dorney Court, Windsor,
Berkshire SL4 6QP

ELY CATHEDRAL
Open in summer from 7am–
7pm; in winter from 7.30am–
6pm (Monday to Saturday),
7.30am–5pm (Sunday).
01353 667 735
www.elycathedral.org
Ely Cathedral, Chapter
House, The College, Ely,
Cambs CB7 4DL

FORDE ABBEY
AND GARDENS
The House is open Tuesdays,
Wednesdays, Thursdays,
Fridays, Sundays and Bank
Holiday Mondays from
12noon–4pm, from 30th
March until 31st October.
Gardens open throughout
the year from 10am.
01460 220 231
www.fordeabbey.co.uk
Forde Abbey, Chard
Somerset TA20 4LU

GLYNDE
01273 858 224
www.glynde.co.uk
The Estate Office, Glynde Place
Gynde, East Sussex BN8 6SX

GODOLPHIN
The Estate is open daily all
year. 'Hard-hat' tours of the
house will be available on
a regular basis through the
season. Please phone for
more information.
01736 763 194
www.nationaltrust.org.uk
Godolphin Cross, Helston,
Cornwall, TR13 9RE

GREAT COXWELL BARN
Open every day, dawn till dusk,
all year round.
01793 762 209
www.nationaltrust.org.uk
Great Coxwell, Faringdon,
Oxfordshire SN7 7LZ

GREAT DIXTER
House and Gardens open
1st April to 31st October,
Tuesdays to Sundays and Bank
Holiday Mondays. Gardens
11am–5pm. House 2pm–5pm.
01797 252 878
www.greatdixter.co.uk
**Great Dixter, Northiam, Rye,
East Sussex TN31 6PH**

HEALE
Open 1st February to 31st
October, 10am–5pm,
Wednesday to Sunday, and Bank
Holidays. No dogs allowed.
01722 782 504
www.healegarden.co.uk
**Heale House. Middle Woodford,
Salisbury, Wiltshire SP4 6NT**

IGHTHAM MOTE
House opening times:
13th March to 31st October 2010,
from 11am–5pm, Thursday to
Monday. 4th November to 19th
December 2010, from 11am–
3pm, Thursday to Sunday.
The estate is open all year.
01732 811 145
www.nationaltrust.org.uk
**Mote Road, Ivy Hatch,
Sevenoaks, Kent TN15 0NT**

KELMSCOTT
Open from April to September
on Wednesdays, 11am to 5pm,
and the first and third
Saturdays of the month.
01367 252 486
www.kelmscottmanor.org.uk
**Kelmscott Manor, Kelmscott,
Lechlade, Glos GL7 3HJ**

KENSAL GREEN CEMETERY
Open every Sunday, March to
October. Guided tours at 2pm.
November to February, open
the first and third Sunday of
every month.
www.kensalgreen.co.uk

LEIGHTON HALL
01524 734 474
www.leightonhall.co.uk

LIBERTY
0207 734 1234
www.liberty.co.uk

LITTLE GIDDING
www.littlegiddingchurch.org.uk

LIVERPOOL CATHEDRAL
Open daily, 8am–6pm.
liverpoolcathedral.org.uk

LYDNEY
01594 842 844 or 01594 842 922
www.lydneyparkestate.co.uk
**Lydney Park Estate,
Lydney Park, Lydney,
Gloucestershire GL15 6BU**

MAPPERTON
All Saint's Church and gardens
open daily (except Saturdays),
1st March to 31st October,
11am–5pm. House open weekdays, 21st June to 30th July,
plus 31st May and 30th August,
2pm–4.30pm. Booking is
advisable. No dogs allowed.
01308 862 645
www.mapperton.com
**Mapperton Gardens,
Beaminster, Dorset DT8 3NR**

PETO GARDEN
From May to September: daily
between 2pm–5pm, except on
Mondays and Fridays.
April and October: Sundays
and Easter Monday, 2pm–5pm.
01225 863 146
www.ifordmanor.co.uk
**Iford Manor, Bradford on
Avon, Wiltshire BA15 2BA**

ROUSHAM
Rousham Gardens are open
every day from 10am.
Last admission at 4.30pm.
The gardens close at dusk.
No dogs allowed.
01869 347 110
www.rousham.org
**Rousham, Bicester,
Oxfordshire OX25 4QU**

SHOBDON CHURCH
www.shobdonchurch.org.uk
**Shobdon Church, Leominster
Herefordshire HR6 9LZ**

SLEDMERE
Open 2nd April to 26th
September, Tuesday to Sunday.
Grounds 10am–5pm.
House 11am–4pm.
01377 236 637
www.sledmerehouse.com
**Sledmere House, Driffield,
East Yorkshire, YO25 3XG**

SOANE MUSEUM
Open Tuesday to Saturday
from 10am–5pm, and from
6pm–9pm on the first Tuesday
of every month.
020 7440 4263
www.soane.org
**Soane Museum
13 Lincoln's Inn Fields,
London WC2A 3BP**
020 7405 2107

SOUTHWELL CATHEDRAL
01636 812 649
www.southwellminster.co.uk
**The Minster Chambers,
Church St, Southwell
NG25 0HD**

PORT ELIOT
Open March to June from
2pm–6pm, except Fridays.
01503 230 211
www.porteliot.co.uk
**Port Eliot Estate Office,
St Germans, Saltash,
Cornwall PL12 5ND**

STANWAY
Open June to August, Tuesdays
and Thursdays, from 2pm–5pm.
01386 584 469
www.stanwayfountain.co.uk
**Stanway House, Stanway
Cheltenham, Gloucestershire
GL54 5P**

TISSINGTON HALL
01335 352 200
www.tissington-hall.com
**Tissington Hall, Tissington,
Ashbourne, DE6 1RA**

TRING MUSEUM
Open Monday to Saturday,
10am–5pm, and Sundays from
2pm–5pm. Except 24th–26th
December.
020 7942 6171
www.nhm.ac.uk
**Natural History Museum at
Tring, The Walter Rothschild
Building, Akeman Street,
Tring, Hertfordshire
HP23 6AP**

BOLTON CASTLE,
WENSLEYDALE
Open 27th March to
31st October, Tuesday to
Sunday, 10am–5pm.
Last admission 4.15pm.
Please phone or see website
for winter opening times.
01969 623 981
www.boltoncastle.co.uk
**Bolton Castle, Nr Leyburn,
North Yorkshire DL8 4ET**

WILTON'S MUSIC HALL
020 7702 2789
www.wiltons.org.uk
**Wilton's, Graces Alley,
Off Ensign Street,
London E1 8JB**

ST MARY'S CHURCH,
WREAY
www.stmaryswreay.org

Photograph and illustration credits